KU-485-941

BUILDING JERUSALEM

A SCRAPBOOK OF
BRITAIN DURING THE
INDUSTRIAL REVOLUTION

"Coalbrookdale by Night" by Philip de Loutherbourg

BUILDING JERUSALEM

A SCRAPBOOK OF BRITAIN DURING THE INDUSTRIAL REVOLUTION

P.R. & J.P. ALDRIDGE

BLACKIE

Blackie & Son Limited
Bishopbriggs, Glasgow G64 2NZ
450/452 Edgware Road, London W2 1EG

© Pauline and Jeffrey Aldridge 1976
First published 1976

Educational Edition ISBN 0 216 89910 9
General Edition ISBN 0 216 89932 X

All rights reserved.
No part of this publication may be reproduced,
stored in a retrieval system, or transmitted
in any form or by any means, electronic,
mechanical, recording or otherwise,
without the prior permission of
Blackie & Son Limited.

Printed in Great Britain
by Robert MacLehose and Company Limited, Glasgow

Foreword

The century from 1750 to 1850 has been called the Age of Revolutions. In France and America the revolutions were political; it is usual to say that in Britain the revolution was industrial. This is true, of course, but it in no way tells the whole story; no society can undergo such a transformation without its whole structure being affected. In this book, we have collected together material from the time in an attempt to show something of this transformation, of the effects on people's lives of this period of rapid and fundamental change.

While there had been rich and poor previously, the two classes had remained intimately linked within the small communities that made up most of British society. With industrialization, however, the two were increasingly separated and alienated from each other. Thus, it was a society of enormous contrasts.

These contrasts we show with the details of domestic life, with the attitudes towards education of the rich and the poor, with the amusements and diversions of different classes, amusements which reflect, in one or two instances, the other significant revolution of the time, that in the arts, represented in Britain in painting and literature.

The working conditions at the beginning of the Industrial Revolution heightened rather than diminished the contrasts in society and sparked off the unrest, the machine-breaking, the cries for reform, which suggested to many that Britain would follow France into political revolution. Repression was severe, however, as the events at Peterloo showed, but reform, in part at least, did come. While the improvements thus introduced were few and limited, they were a beginning. The period covered in this book was not only the beginning of industrialization; it also set the stage for the beginning of liberalization.

PAULINE AND JEFFREY ALDRIDGE

Acknowledgments

For permission to reproduce copyright material in this anthology, the compilers and publishers would like to thank the following:

The Science Museum, London, for the painting used as a frontispiece and the engraving at the top of page 47.

The Print Department of the Boston Public Library for the watercolour drawings on pages 4 and 6.

The Trustees of the British Museum for the cartoons on pages 15, 33, 72 and 81, and the lithograph on page 24.

Mary Evans Picture Library for the engraving on page 19.

Marylebone Cricket Club for the painting on page 40.

The Tate Gallery, London, for the painting on page 41.

The Walker Art Gallery, Liverpool, for the painting on page 52.

The John Frost Historical Newspaper Service for the facsimile on page 83.

H.M. The Queen for the painting on page 84.

Every effort has been made to trace copyright holders, but in some cases this has not been possible. The publishers would, however, be glad to hear from any copyright holders not included.

Contents

Prologue

"How little can the rich man know
 Of what the poor man feels,
When Want, like some dark demon foe,
 Nearer and nearer steals!

He never tramp'd the weary round,
 A stroke of work to gain,
And sicken'd at the dreaded sound
 Which tells he seeks in vain.

Foot-sore, heart-sore, *he* never came
 Back through the winter's wind,
To a dank cellar, there no flame,
 No light, no food, to find.

He never saw his darlings lie
 Shivering, the flags their bed;
He never heard that maddening cry,
 'Daddy, a bit of bread!' "

Manchester song from *Mary Barton* by Mrs Gaskell

The Eating Habits of the English Aristocracy
(A French view from the late eighteenth century)

Dinner is one of the most wearisome of English experiences, lasting, as it does, for four or five hours. The first two are spent in eating and you are compelled to exercise your stomach to the full in order to please your host. He asks you the whole time whether you like the food and presses you to eat more, with the result that, out of pure politeness, I do nothing but eat from the time that I sit down until the time when I get up from the table.

The courses are much the same as in France except that the use of sauce is unknown in the English kitchen and that one seldom sees a *ragout*. All the dishes consist of various meats either boiled or roasted and of joints weighing about twenty or thirty pounds.

After the sweets, you are given water in small bowls of very clean glass in order to rinse out your mouth—a custom which strikes me as extremely unfortunate. The more fashionable folk do not rinse out their mouths, but that seems to me even worse; for if you use the water to wash your hands, it becomes dirty and quite disgusting. This ceremony over, the cloth is removed and you behold the most beautiful table that it is possible to see. It is indeed remarkable that the English are so much given to the use of mahogany; not only are their tables generally made of it, but also their doors and seats and the handrails of their staircases. Yet it is just as dear in England as in France. It is a matter which I do not pretend to understand, but I am inclined to think that the English must be richer than we are; certainly I have myself observed not only that everything costs twice as much here as in France but that the English seize every opportunity to use things which are expensive in themselves. At all events, their tables are made of the most beautiful wood and always have a brilliant polish like that of the finest glass. After the removal of the cloth, the table is covered with all kinds of wine, for even gentlemen of modest means always keep a large stock of good wine. On the middle of the table there is a small quantity of fruit, a few biscuits (to stimulate thirst) and some butter, for many English people take it at dessert.

At this point all the servants disappear. The ladies drink a glass or two of wine and at the end of half an hour all go out together. It is then that real enjoyment begins—there is not an Englishman who is not supremely happy at this particular moment. One proceeds to drink—sometimes in an alarming measure. Everyone has to drink in his turn, for the bottles make a continuous circuit of the table and the host takes note that everyone is drinking in his turn. After this has gone on for some time and when thirst has become an inadequate reason for drinking, a fresh stimulus is supplied by the drinking of "toasts", that is to say, the host begins by giving the name of a lady; he drinks to her health and everyone is obliged to do likewise. After the host, someone else gives a toast and everyone drinks to the health of everyone else's lady. Then each member of the party names some man and the whole ceremony begins again. If more drinking is required, fresh toasts are always ready to hand; politics can supply plenty—one drinks to the health of Mr. Pitt or Mr. Fox or Lord North. This is the time that I like best: Conversation is as free as it can be, everyone expresses his political opinions with as much frankness as he would employ upon personal subjects. Sometimes conversation becomes extremely free upon highly indecent topics—complete licence is allowed and I have come to the conclusion that the English do not associate the same ideas with certain words that we do. Very often I have heard things mentioned in good society which would be in the grossest taste in France. The sideboard too is furnished with a number of chamber pots and it is a common practice to relieve oneself whilst the rest are drinking; one has no kind of concealment and the practice strikes me as most indecent.

At the end of two or three hours a servant announces that tea is ready and conducts the gentlemen from their drinking to join the ladies in the drawing-room, where they are usually employed in making tea and coffee. After making tea, one generally plays whist, and at midnight there is cold meat for those who are hungry. While the game is going on, there is punch on a table for those who want it.

M. de Liancourt

3

"An Eating House" by Thomas Rowlandson

The Labourer's Table

The usual breakfast of a labourer, in this part of the world, is broth, made of coarse ends of beef, with oatmeal flour and butter; or boiled milk; or bread and cheese. His dinner is sometimes pork and bacon. His supper, bread and milk and cheese; new milk half a pint. Good fare.

from *General View of the Agriculture of Sussex*, 1808, by Arthur Young

The population employed in the cotton factories rises at five o'clock in the morning, works in the mills from six till eight o'clock, and returns home for half an hour or forty minutes to breakfast. This meal generally consists of tea or coffee with a little bread. Oatmeal porridge is sometimes, but of late rarely used, and chiefly by the men; but the stimulus of tea is preferred, and especially by the women. The tea is almost always of a bad, and sometimes of a deleterious quality, the infusion is weak, and little or no milk is added. The operatives return to the mills and workshops until twelve o'clock, when an hour is allowed for dinner. Amongst those who obtain the lower rates of wages this meal generally consists of boiled potatoes. The mess of potatoes is put into one large dish; melted lard and butter are poured upon them, and a few pieces of fried fat bacon are sometimes mingled with them, and but seldom a little meat. Those who obtain better wages, or families whose aggregate income is larger, add a greater proportion of animal food to this meal, at least three times in the week; but the quantity consumed by the labouring population is not great. The family sits round the table, and each rapidly appropriates his portion on a plate, or, they all plunge their spoons into the dish, and with an animal eagerness satisfy the cravings of their appetite.

from *The Moral and Physical Conduct of the Working Classes employed in the Cotton Manufacture in Manchester*, 1832, by J. P. Kay

There is not only a remarkable difference in the proportion of earnings appropriated to the purchase of subsistence by labourers in the North and South of England; but their mode of preparing their food is no less dissimilar. In the South of England, the poorest labourers are habituated to the unvarying meal of dry bread and cheese from one week's end: and in those families, whose finances do not allow them the indulgence of malt liquor, the deleterious produce of China (tea) constitutes their most usual and general beverage. If a labourer is rich enough to afford himself meat once a week, he commonly adopts the simplest of all culinary preparations; that of roasting it; or, if he lives near a baker's, of baking it; and if he boils his meat, he never thinks of forming it into a soup, that would not only be as wholesome, and as nourishing, but, certainly, more palatable than a plain boiled joint.

In the North of England, and in Scotland and Wales, on the contrary, the poorest labourers can, and actually do, regale themselves with a variety of dishes that are wholly unknown to the Southern inhabitant of this island . . . To begin with one of the simplest articles of diet, "the healsome porritch, chief of Scotia's food", hasty-pudding . . . is extremely nutritious . . . *Crowdie* is not so generally used as hasty-pudding. It is, however, a very common dish in the North, among labourers of all descriptions, but particularly miners, as it is soon made ready, and without much trouble. The process is extremely simple; and consists in pouring boiling water over oat-meal and stirring it a little. (Broth or corned beef may be added.)

from *The State of the Poor*, 1797, by Sir F. M. Eden

"Market Day" by Thomas Rowlandson

Apology for the Poor

Mr Editor

In this suprising stir of patrioutism and wonderful change in the ways and opinions of men when your paper is weekly loaded with the free speechs of county meetings can you find room for mine ? or will you hear the voice of a poor man ?—I only wish to ask you a few plain questions.

Amidst all this stir about taxation and tythes and agricultural distress are the poor to recieve corresponding benefits   they have been told so I know but it is not the first time they have heard that and been dissapointed   when the tax was taken from leather they was told they should have shoes almost for nothing and they heard the parliment speeches of patriots as the forthcoming propechys of a political millenium but their hopes were soon frost bitten for the tax has long vanished and the price of shoes remains just were it did   nay I believe they are a trifle dearer then they was then— thats the only difference   then there was a hue and cry about taking off the duty of Spritous liquors and the best Gin was to be little more in price then small beer   the poor man shook his head over such speeches and looking at his shoes had no faith to believe any more of these cheap wonders so he was not dissapointed in finding gin as dear as ever—for which he had little to regret for he prefered good ale to any spirits   and now the Malt and beer tax is in full cry what is the poor man to expect   it may benefit the farmers a little and the common brewers a good deal and there no doubt the matter will end   the poor man will not find the refuse of any more use to him than a dry bone to a hungry dog—excuse the simile reader for the poor have been likened unto dogs before now   and many other of these time serving hue and cries might be noticed in which the poor man was promised as much benefit as the stork was in the fable for pulling out the bone from the Wolfs throat and who got just as much at last as the stork for his pains.

from a letter by John Clare, c. 1829

Song to the Men of England

Men of England, wherefore plough
For the lords who lay ye low?
Wherefore weave with toil and care
The rich robes your tyrants wear?

Wherefore feed, and clothe, and save,
From the cradle to the grave,
Those ungrateful drones who would
Drain your sweat—nay, drink your blood?

Wherefore, Bees of England, forge
Many a weapon, chain, and scourge,
That these stingless drones may spoil
The forced produce of your toil?

Have ye leisure, comfort, calm,
Shelter, food, love's gentle balm?
Or what is it ye buy so dear
With your pain and with your fear?

The seed ye sow, another reaps:
The wealth ye find, another keeps;
The robes ye weave, another wears;
The arms ye forge, another bears.

Sow seed,—but let no tyrant reap;
Find wealth,—let no impostor heap;
Weave robes,—let not the idle wear;
Forge arms,—in your defence to bear.

Shrink to your cellars, holes, and cells;
In halls ye deck another dwells.
Why shake ye chains ye wrought? Ye see
The steel ye tempered glance on ye.

With plough and spade, and hoe and loom,
Trace your grave, and build your tomb,
And weave your winding-sheet, till fair
England be your sepulchre.

Percy Bysshe Shelley

Class Differences

They met Mr. Martin the very next day, as they were walking on the Donwell Road. He was on foot, and after looking very respectfully at her, looked with most unfeigned satisfaction at her companion. Emma was not sorry to have such an opportunity of survey; and walking a few yards forward, while they talked together, soon made her quick eye sufficiently acquainted with Mr. Robert Martin. His appearance was very neat, and he looked like a sensible young man, but his person had no other advantage; and when he came to be contrasted with gentlemen, she thought he must lose all the ground he had gained in Harriet's inclination. Harriet was not insensible of manner; she had voluntarily noticed her father's gentleness with admiration as well as wonder. Mr. Martin looked as if he did not know what manner was.

They remained but a few minutes together, as Miss Woodhouse must not be kept waiting; and Harriet then came running to her with a smiling face, and in a flutter of spirits, which Miss Woodhouse hoped very soon to compose.

"Only think of our happening to meet him!—How very odd! . . . Well, Miss Woodhouse, is he like what you expected? What do you think of him? Do you think him so very plain?"

"He is very plain, undoubtedly—remarkably plain:—but that is nothing, compared with his entire want of gentility. I had no right to expect much, and I did not expect much; but I had no idea that he could be so very clownish, so totally without air. I had imagined him, I confess, a degree or two nearer gentility."

"To be sure," said Harriet, in a mortified voice, "he is not so genteel as real gentlemen."

"I think, Harriet, since your acquaintance with us, you have been repeatedly in the company of some, such very real gentlemen, that you must yourself be struck with the difference in Mr. Martin. At Hartfield you have had very good specimens of well educated, well bred men. I should be surprised if, after seeing them, you could be in company with Mr. Martin again without perceiving him to be a very inferior creature—and rather wondering at yourself for having ever thought him at all agreeable before. Do not you begin to feel that now? Were you not struck? I am sure you must have been struck by his awkward look and abrupt manner—and the uncouthness of a voice, which I heard to be wholly unmodulated as I stood here."

"Certainly, he is not like Mr. Knightley. He has not such a fine air and way of walking as Mr. Knightley. I see the difference plain enough. But Mr. Knightley is so very fine a man!

"Mr. Knightley's air is so remarkably good, that it is not fair to compare Mr. Martin with *him*. You might not see one in a hundred, with *gentleman* so plainly written as in Mr. Knightley. But he is not the only gentleman you have been lately used to. What say you to Mr. Weston and Mr. Elton? Compare Mr. Martin with either of *them*. Compare their manner of carrying themselves; of walking; of speaking; of being silent. You must see the difference."

"Oh, yes!—there is a great difference. But Mr. Weston is almost an old man. Mr. Weston must be between forty and fifty."

"Which makes his good manners the more valuable. The older a person grows, Harriet, the more important it is that their manners should not be bad—the more glaring and disgusting any loudness, or coarseness, or awkwardness becomes. What is passable in youth, is detestable in later age. Mr. Martin is now awkward and abrupt; what will he be at Mr. Weston's time of life?"

"There is no saying indeed!" replied Harriet, rather solemnly.

"But there may be pretty good guessing. He will be a completely gross, vulgar farmer—totally inattentive to appearances, and thinking of nothing but profit and loss."

"Will he, indeed, that will be very bad."

"How much his business engrosses him already, is very plain from the circumstances of his forgetting to inquire for the book you recommended. He was a great deal too full of the market to think of any thing else—which is just as it should be, for a thriving man. What has he to do with books? And I have no doubt that he *will* thrive and be a very rich man in time—and his being illiterate and coarse need not disturb *us*."

from *Emma*, 1814, by Jane Austen

The Desertion of the Countryside

Sweet smiling village, loveliest of the lawn,
Thy sports are fled, and all thy charms withdrawn;
Amidst thy bowers the tyrant's hand is seen,
And desolation saddens all the green:
One only master grasps the whole domain,
And half a tillage stints thy smiling plain;
No more thy glassy brook reflects the day,
But choked with sedges, works its weedy way;
Along thy glades, a solitary guest,
The hollow sounding bittern guards its nest;
Amidst thy desert walks the lapwing flies,
And tires their echoes with unvaried cries.
Sunk are thy bowers, in shapeless ruin all,
And the long grass o'ertops the mouldering wall;
And trembling, shrinking from the spoiler's hand,
Far, far away thy children leave the land.

*   *   *

Near yonder thorn, that lifts its head on high,
Where once the sign-post caught the passing eye,
Low lies the house where nut-brown draughts inspired,
Where grey-beard mirth and smiling toil retired,
Where village statesmen talked with looks profound,
And news much older than their ale went round.
Imagination fondly stoops to trace
The parlour splendours of that festive place;
The white-washed wall, the nicely sanded floor,
The varnished clock that clicked behind the door;
The chest contrived a double debt to pay,
A bed by night, a chest of drawers by day;
The pictures placed for ornament and use,
The twelve good rules, the royal game of goose;
The hearth, except when winter chill'd the day,
With aspen boughs, and flowers, and fennel gay,
While broken tea-cups, wisely kept for show,
Ranged o'er the chimney, glistened in a row.

Vain transitory splendours! Could not all
Reprieve the tottering mansion from its fall!
Obscure it sinks, nor shall it more impart
An hour's importance to the poor man's heart;
Thither no more the peasant shall repair
To sweet oblivion of his daily care;
No more the farmer's news, the barber's tale,
No more the wood-man's ballad shall prevail;
No more the smith his dusky brow shall clear,
Relax his ponderous strength, and lean to hear;
The host himself no longer shall be found
Careful to see the mantling bliss go round;
Nor the coy maid, half willing to be prest,
Shall kiss the cup to pass it to the rest.

from *The Deserted Village*, 1770, by Oliver Goldsmith

Cheltenham

. . . Here we come to one of the devouring WENS; namely,
CHELTENHAM, which is what they call a *"watering place"*; that
is to say, a place, to which East India plunderers, West India
floggers, English tax-gorgers, together with gluttons, drunkards,
and debauchees of all descriptions, *female* as well as male, resort, at
the suggestion of silently laughing quacks, in the hope of getting
rid of the bodily consequences of their manifold sins and iniquities.
When I enter a place like this, I always feel disposed to squeeze up
my nose with my fingers. It is nonsense, to be sure; but I conceit
that every two-legged creature, that I see coming near me, is about
to cover me with the poisonous proceeds of its impurities. To places
like this come all that is knavish and all that is foolish and all that is
base; gamesters, pick-pockets, and harlots; young wife-hunters in
search of rich and ugly and old women, and young husband-
hunters in search of rich and wrinkled or half-rotten men . . .

from *Rural Rides* (entry for 30th September, 1826) by William Cobbett

"Round Dance" by Thomas Rowlandson

An Evening at the Brighton Pavilion

Oh this wicked Pavillion! we were there till ½ past one this morning,
and it has kept me in bed with the headache till 12 today. The in-
vitation did not come to us till 9 o'clock: we went in Lord Thurlow's
carriage, and were in fear of being too late; but the Prince did not
come out of the dining-room till 11. Till then our only companions
were Lady Downshire and Mr. and Miss Johnstone—the former
very goodnatured and amiable. When the Prince appeared, I
instantly saw he had got more wine than usual, and it was still more
evident that the German Baron was extremely drunk. The Prince
came up and sat by me—introduced McMahon to me. . . .

It appears to me I have found a true friend in Mac. He is even
more foolish than I expected; but I shall be disappointed if, even
to you, he does not profess himself my devoted admirer.

Afterwards the Prince led all the party to the table where the
maps lie, to see him shoot with an air-gun at a target placed at the
end of the room. He did it very skilfully, and wanted all the ladies
to attempt it. The girls and I excused ourselves on account of our

short sight; but Lady Downshire hit a fiddler in the dining-room, Miss Johnstone a door and Bloomfield the ceiling. I soon had enough of this, and retired to the fire with Mac . . . At last a waltz was played by the band, and the Prince offered to waltz with Miss Johnstone, but very quietly, and once round the table made him giddy, so of course it was proper for his partner to be giddy too; but he cruelly only thought of supporting himself, so she reclined on the Baron.

from a letter by Mrs Creevey to her husband, 29th October, 1805

George the Fourth

He left an example for age and for youth
To avoid.
He never acted well by Man or Woman,
And was as false to his Mistress as to his Wife.
He deserted his Friends and his Principles.
He was so ignorant that he could scarcely Spell;
But he had some Skill in Cutting out Coats,
And an undeniable Taste for Cookery.
He built the Palaces of Brighton and of Buckingham,
And for these Qualities and Proofs of Genius,
An admiring Aristocracy
Christened him the "First Gentleman in Europe".
Friends, respect the King whose Statue is here,
And the generous Aristocracy who admired him.

William Makepeace Thackeray (from *Punch*, 1845)

"A Voluptuary Under the Horrors of Digestion" by James Gillray
(The Prince of Wales lingers over a meal at Carlton House)

Edinburgh

Edinburgh in 1763 was almost entirely confined within the city walls. The suburbs were of small extent. To the north, there was no bridge; and (till of late) the New Town, with all its elegant and magnificent buildings, squares, rows, courts, etc., extending upwards of a mile in length and near half a mile in breadth, did not exist.

It may with truth be said, that there is not now in Europe a more beautiful terrace than Prince's Street, nor a more elegant street than George Street. The views from Queen Street, to the north, exhibit a scene of grandeur and beauty unparalleled in any city.

It is a moderate calculation to say, that three millions sterling have been expended on buildings and public improvements in and about the city of Edinburgh since 1763, the environs of which cannot be surpassed in views of the sublime, the picturesque, and the beautiful.

In 1763 people of quality and fashion lived in houses which in 1783 were inhabited by tradesmen, or by people in humble and ordinary life.

Wonders of Coach Travel

In 1763, there were two stage-coaches, with three horses, a coachman, and postilion to each coach, which went to the port of Leith (a mile and a half distant) every hour from eight in the morning till eight at night, and consumed a full hour upon the road. There were no other stage-coaches in Scotland except one, which set out once a month for London, and it was from twelve to sixteen days upon the journey.

In 1783 there were five or six stage-coaches to Leith every half-hour, which ran it in fifteen minutes. There are now stage-coaches, flies and diligences, to every considerable town in Scotland, and to many of them two, three, four and five. To London there were no less than sixty stage-coaches monthly, or fifteen every week, and they reached the capital in four days . . .

A person may now set out on Sunday afternoon, after divine service, from Edinburgh to London; may stay a whole day in London, and be again in Edinburgh on Saturday at six in the morning! The distance from Edinburgh to London is 400 miles.

Forty years ago it was common for people to make their will before setting out on a London journey. . . .

Servants

In 1763, the wages to maid-servants were generally from £3 to £4 a year. They dressed decently in red or blue cloaks, or in plaids, suitable to their station. In 1783, the wages are nearly the same; but their dress and appearance are greatly altered, the maid-servants dressing almost as fine as their mistresses did in 1763.

In 1763, few families had men-servants. The wages were from £6 to £10 per annum. In 1783, almost every genteel family had a man-servant, and the wages were from £10 to £20 a year.

Public Dances

In 1763, there was one dancing assembly-room, the profits of which went to the support of the charity-workhouse. Minuets were danced by each set previous to the country dances. Strict regularity with respect to dress and decorum, and great dignity of manners were observed. The company met at five o'clock in the afternoon, and the dancing began at six and ended at eleven, by public orders of the manager, which were never transgressed.

In 1783 they met at eight and nine o'clock, and the Lady Directress sometimes did not make her appearance till ten. The young masters and misses, who would have been mortified not to have seen out the ball, thus returned home at three and four in the morning, and yawned and gaped and complained of headache all the next day.

In 1786 there were three new elegant assembly-rooms at Edinburgh, besides one at Leith, but the charity-workhouse was unprovided for to the extent of its necessities. Minuets were given up and country dances only used, which had often a nearer resemblance to a game of romps than to elegant and graceful dancing. Dress, particularly by the men, was much neglected; and many of them reeled from the tavern, flustered with wine, to an assembly of as elegant and beautiful women as any in Europe.

Sunday Behaviour

In 1763, it was fashionable to go to church, and people were interested about religion. Sunday was strictly observed by all ranks as a day of devotion; and it was disgraceful to be seen upon the streets during the time of public worship. Families attended church, with their children and servants; and family worship was frequent. In 1783, attendance at church was neglected, particularly by the men. Sunday was by many made a day of relaxation; and young people were allowed to stroll about at all hours. Families thought it ungenteel to take their domestics to church with them.

Women of the Town

In 1763, there were five or six brothels, or houses of bad fame, and a very few of the lowest and most ignorant order of female skulked about the streets at night. A person might have gone from the Castle to Holyroodhouse (the then length of the city) at any hour of the night, without being accosted by a single street-walker. In 1783, the number of brothels had increased twenty-fold, and the women of the town more than a hundred-fold. Every quarter of the city and suburbs was infested with multitudes of females abandoned to vice, and a great many at a very early period of life, before passion could mislead, or reason teach them right from wrong.

Crime and Punishment

In 1763, house-breaking and robbery were extremely rare. Many thought it unnecessary to lock their doors at night. In 1783, 1784, 1785, 1786, and 1787, house-breaking, theft, and robbery were astonishingly frequent; and many of these crimes were committed by boys, whose age prevented them from being made objects of capital punishment. The culprits were uniformly apprehended in houses of bad fame, in which they were protected and encouraged in their depredations on the public.

In 1763, and many years preceding and following, the execution of criminals was rare: three annually were reckoned the average for the whole kingdom of Scotland. There were three succeeding years (1774–6) in which there was not an execution in Edinburgh. In 1783 there were six criminals under sentence of death in Edinburgh jail, in one week; and upon the autumn circuit, no less than thirty-seven capital indictments were issued.

from *Fugitive Pieces*, 1815, by William Creech

Dirty Father Thames

Filthy river, filthy river,
    Foul from London to the Nore,
What art thou but one vast gutter,
    One tremendous common shore?

All beside thy sludgy waters,
    All beside thy reeking ooze,
Christian folks inhale mephitis,
    Which thy bubbly bosom brews.

All her foul abominations
    Into thee the City throws;
These pollutions, ever churning,
    To and fro thy current flows.

And from thee is brew'd our porter—
    Thee, thou gully, puddle, sink!
Thou, vile cesspool, art the liquor
    Whence is made the beer we drink!

Thou, too, hast a Conservator,
    He who fills the civic chair;
Well does he conserve thee, truly,
    Does he not, my good LORD MAYOR?

Anonymous (from Punch, 1848)

The Thames with Blackfriar's Bridge and St. Paul's in the background

Manchester

Thirty or forty factories rise on the tops of the hills . . . Their six stories tower up; their huge enclosures give notice from afar of the centralization of industry. The wretched dwellings of the poor are scattered haphazard around them. Round them stretches land uncultivated but without the charm of rustic nature, and still without the amenities of a town. The soil has been taken away, scratched and torn up in a thousand places, but it is not yet covered with the habitations of men. The land is given over to industry's use. The roads which connect the still-disjointed limbs of the great city, show, like the rest, every sign of hurried and unfinished work; the incidental activity of a population bent on gain, which seeks to amass gold so as to have everything else all at once, and, in the interval, mistrusts all the niceties of life. Some of these roads are paved, but most of them are full of ruts and puddles into which foot or carriage wheel sinks deep. Heaps of dung, rubble from buildings, putrid, stagnant pools are found here and there among the houses and over the bumpy, pitted surfaces of the public places. No trace of surveyor's rod or spirit level. Amid this noisome labyrinth, this great sombre stretch of brickwork, from time to time one is astonished at the sight of fine stone buildings with Corinthian columns. It might be a medieval town with the marvels of the nineteenth century in the middle of it. But who could describe the interiors of these quarters set apart, home of vice and poverty, which surround the huge palaces of industry and clasp them in their hideous folds. On ground below the level of the river and over-shadowed on every side by immense workshops, stretches marshy land which widely spaced ditches can neither drain nor cleanse. Narrow, twisting roads lead down to it. They are lined with one-storey houses whose ill-fitting planks and broken windows show them up, even from a distance, as the last refuge a man might find between poverty and death. None-the-less the wretched people living in them can still inspire jealousy of their fellow-beings. Below some of their miserable dwellings is a row of cellars to which a sunken corridor leads. Twelve to fifteen human beings are crowded pell-mell into each of these damp, repulsive holes.

The fetid, muddy waters, stained with a thousand colours by the factories they pass . . . wander slowly round this refuge of poverty. They are nowhere kept in place by quays: houses are built haphazard on their banks. Often from the top of one of their steep banks one sees an attempt at a road opening out through the debris of earth, and the foundations of some houses or the debris of others. It is the Styx of this new Hades. Look up and all around this place and you will see the huge palaces of industry. You will hear the noise of furnaces, the whistle of steam. These vast structures keep air and light out of the human habitations which they dominate; they envelope them in perpetual fog; here is the slave, there the master; there is the wealth of some, here the poverty of most; there the organized efforts of thousands produce, to the profit of one man, what society has not yet learnt to give. Here the weakness of the individual seems more feeble and helpless even than in the middle of a wilderness.

A sort of black smoke covers the city. The sun seen through it is a disc without rays. Under this half-daylight 300,000 human beings are ceaselessly at work. A thousand noises disturb this dark, damp labyrinth, but they are not at all the ordinary sounds one hears in great cities.

The footsteps of a busy crowd, the crunching wheels of machinery, the shriek of steam from boilers, the regular beat of the looms, the heavy rumble of carts, those are the noises from which you can never escape in the sombre half-light of these streets. You will never hear the clatter of hoofs as the rich man drives back home or out on expeditions of pleasure. Never the gay shouts of people amusing themselves, or music heralding a holiday. You will never see smart folk strolling at leisure in the streets, or going out on innocent pleasure parties in the surrounding country. Crowds are ever hurrying this way and that in the Manchester streets, but their footsteps are brisk, their looks preoccupied, and their appearance sombre and harsh. . . .

From this foul drain the greatest stream of human industry flows out to fertilize the whole world. From this filthy sewer pure gold flows. Here humanity attains its most complete development and its most brutish; here civilization makes its miracles, and civilized man is turned back almost into a savage.

from *Journeys to England and Ireland*, 1835, by Alexis de Tocqueville

Industrial Landscape

The child walked with more difficulty than she had led her companion to expect, for the pains that racked her joints were of no common severity, and every exertion increased them. But they wrung from her no complaint, or look of suffering; and, though the two travellers proceeded very slowly, they did proceed; and clearing the town in course of time, began to feel that they were fairly on their way.

A long suburb of red brick houses,—some with patches of garden-ground, where coal-dust and factory smoke darkened the shrinking leaves, and coarse rank flowers; and where the struggling vegetation sickened and sank under the hot breath of kiln and furnace, making them by its presence seem yet more blighting and unwholesome than in the town itself,—a long, flat, straggling suburb passed, they came by slow degrees upon a cheerless region, where not a blade of grass was seen to grow; where not a bud put forth its promise in the spring; where nothing green could live but on the surface of the stagnant pools, which here and there lay idly sweltering by the black roadside.

Advancing more and more into the shadow of this mournful place, its dark depressing influence stole upon their spirits, and filled them with a dismal gloom. On every side, and far as the eye could see into the heavy distance, tall chimneys, crowding on each other, and presenting that endless repetition of the same dull, ugly form, which is the horror of oppressive dreams, poured out their plague of smoke, obscured the light, and made foul the melancholy air. On mounds of ashes by the wayside, sheltered only by a few rough boards, or rotten pent-house roofs, strange engines spun and writhed like tortured creatures; clanking their iron chains, shrieking in their rapid whirl from time to time as though in torment unendurable, and making the ground tremble with their agonies. Dismantled houses here and there appeared, tottering to the earth, propped up by fragments of others that had fallen down, unroofed, windowless, blackened, desolate, but yet inhabited. Men, women, children, wan in their looks and ragged in attire, tended the engines, fed their tributary fires, begged upon the road, or scowled half-naked from the doorless houses. Then came more of the wrathful monsters, whose like they almost seemed to be in their wildness and their untamed air, screeching and turning round and round again; and still, before, behind, and to the right and left was the same interminable perspective of brick towers, never ceasing in their black vomit, blasting all things living or inanimate, shutting out the face of day, and closing in on all these horrors with a dense dark cloud.

But night-time in this dreadful spot!—night, when the smoke was changed to fire; when every chimney spirted up its flame; and places, that had been dark vaults all day, now shone red-hot, with figures moving to and fro within their blazing jaws, and calling to one another with hoarse cries—night, when the noise of every strange machine was aggravated by the darkness; when the people near them looked wilder and more savage; when bands of unemployed labourers paraded in the roads, or clustered by torch-light round their leaders, who told them in stern language of their wrongs, and urged them on to frightful cries and threats; when maddened men, armed with sword and fire-brand, spurning the tears and prayers of women who would restrain them, rushed forth on errands of terror and destruction, to work no ruin half so surely as their own—night, when carts came rumbling by, filled with rude coffins (for contagious disease and death had been busy with the living crops); when orphans cried, and distracted women shrieked and followed in their wake—night, when some called for bread, and some for drink to drown their cares; and some with tears, and some with staggering feet, and some with bloodshot eyes, went brooding home—night, which, unlike the night that Heaven sends on earth, brought with it no peace, nor quiet, nor signs of blessed sleep—who shall tell the terrors of the night to that young wandering child!

from *The Old Curiosity Shop*, 1841, by Charles Dickens

Explosion and fire at Shiffnal, near Wellington, Shropshire, 1821

The Sweep

One day I fell down a long chimney and broke my leg,
But no one felt for me.
I have a wound in my side, but I have no salve to heal it.
You pity me, little girl!
But hush! I must not even hear the kind words of pity,
   for my master is near, and he will say I complain,
And he will beat me the more.
Oh, I cannot look upon this boy. His pains wring my heart.
Can nothing be done to save him, to ease him,
To snatch him from his hard, hard fate?
Little girl, dry your tears. I have some good news for you.
There will soon be a law, a blessed law that shall stop the pangs of
   the poor sweep.

from *Nursery Morals, Chiefly in Monosyllables*, 1818

A Contract of Apprenticeship

THIS INDENTURE WITNESSETH, That Joseph Ringer, Son of John Ringer of the parish of Thetford in the County of Kent doth put himself Apprentice to John Whiffin of the said parish Wheelwright to learn his Art, and with him (after the Manner of an Apprentice) to serve from the 19th Day of November 1804 unto the full End and Term of three and half Years from thence following, to be fully compleat and ended. During which Term, the said Apprentice his said Master faithfully shall serve, his Secrets keep, his lawful Commands every where gladly do. He shall do no Damage to his said Master, nor see to be done of others, but that he to his Power shall let or forthwith give Warning to his said Master of the same. He shall not waste the Goods of his said Master nor lend them unlawfully to any. He shall not commit Fornication, nor contract Matrimony within the said Term. He shall not play at Cards, Dice, Tables, or any other unlawful Games, whereby his said Master may have any Loss. With his own Goods or others, during the said Term, without Licence of his said Master, he shall neither buy nor sell. He shall not haunt Taverns or Play-houses, nor absent himself from his said Master's Service Day nor Night unlawfully. But in all Things as a faithful Apprentice he shall behave himself towards his said Master and all his during the said Term.

And the said John Ringer shall give unto the said John Whiffin the Sum of Nine pounds Nineteen shillings to Learn his said Apprentice, in the same Art of a Wheelwright, which he useth, by the best Means that he can, shall Teach and Instruct, or cause to be taught and instructed; finding unto his said Apprentice sufficient Meat, Drink, Lodging, and all other Necessaries during the said Term.

And for the true Performance of all and every the said Covenants and Agreements, either of the said Parties bindeth himself unto the other by these Presents. In Witness whereof the Parties above-named to these Indentures interchangeably have put their Hands and Seals, the fifth Day of November in the Forty fourth Year of the Reign of our Sovereign Lord George the Third by the Grace of God of the United Kingdom of Great Britain and Ireland, King, Defender of the Faith,

and in the Year of our Lord One Thousand Eight Hundred and
Four.

Joseph Ringer

Rich. Grey ⎱
Wm. Whiffin ⎰ Witnesses

The Apprentice System

He built a mud-wall'd hovel, where he kept
His various wealth, and there he oft-times slept;
But no success could please his cruel soul,
He wish'd for one to trouble and control;
He wanted some obedient boy to stand
And bear the blow of his outrageous hand;
And hoped to find in some propitious hour
A feeling creature subject to his power.

Peter had heard there were in London then,—
Still have they being!—workhouse-clearing men,
Who, undisturb'd by feelings just or kind,
Would parish-boys to needy tradesmen bind:
They in their want a trifling sum would take,
And toiling slaves of piteous orphans make.

Such Peter sought, and when a lad was found,
The sum was dealt him, and the slave was bound.
Some few in town observed in Peter's trap
A boy, with jacket blue and woollen cap;
But none enquired how Peter used the rope,
Or what the bruise, that made the stripling stoop;
None could the ridges on his back behold,
None sought him shivering in the winter's cold;
None put the question,—"Peter, dost thou give
"The boy his food?—What, man! the lad must live:
"Consider, Peter, let the child have bread,
"He'll serve thee better if he's stroked and fed."
None reason'd thus—and some, on hearing cries,
Said calmly, "Grimes is at his exercise."

Pinn'd, beaten, cold, pinch'd, threaten'd, and abused—
His efforts punish'd and his food refused,—
Awake tormented,—soon aroused from sleep,—
Struck if he wept, and yet compell'd to weep,
The trembling boy dropp'd down and strove to pray,
Or sobb'd and hid his piteous face;—while he,
The savage master, grinn'd in horrid glee:
He'd now the power he ever loved to show,
A feeling being subject to his blow.

Thus lived the lad, in hunger, peril, pain,
His tears despised, his supplications vain:
Compell'd by fear to lie, by need to steal,
His bed uneasy and unbless'd his meal,
For three sad years the boy his tortures bore,
And then his pains and trials were no more.

"How died he, Peter?" when the people said,
He growl'd—"I found him lifeless in his bed;"
Then tried for softer tone, and sigh'd, "Poor Sam is dead."
Yet murmurs were there, and some questions ask'd—
How he was fed, how punish'd, and how task'd?
Much they suspected, but they little proved,
And Peter pass'd untroubled and unmoved.

Another boy with equal ease was found,
The money granted, and the victim bound. . . .

from *Peter Grimes*, 1810, a section of *The Borough*
by George Crabbe

Classical Education

"The principal defect," says Mr. Edgeworth, "in the present system
of our great schools is, that they devote too large a portion of time
to Latin and Greek. It is true, that the attainment of classical literature is highly desirable; but it should not, or rather it need not,
be the exclusive object of boys during eight or nine years . . . Though
. . . parents, and the public in general, may be convinced of the

absurdity of making boys spend so much of life in learning what can be of no use to them; such are the difficulties of making any change in the ancient rules of great establishments, that masters themselves, however reasonable, dare not, and cannot make sudden alterations . . . New schools, that are not restricted to any established routine, should give a fair trial to experiments in education, which afford a rational prospect of success."

. . . A young Englishman goes to school at six or seven years old; and he remains in a course of education till twenty-three or twenty-four years of age. In all that time his sole exclusive occupation is learning Latin and Greek (unless he goes to the University of Cambridge; and then classics occupy him entirely for about ten years; and divide him with mathematics for four of five more): he has scarcely a notion that there is any other kind of excellence; and the great system of facts with which he is the most perfectly acquainted, are the intrigues of the Heathen Gods: with whom Pan slept? with whom Jupiter?—whom Apollo ravished? . . . If you have neglected to put other things in him, they will never get in afterwards;—if you have fed him only with words, he will remain a narrow and limited being to the end of his existence.

. . . A very curious argument is sometimes employed in justification of the learned minutiae to which all young men are doomed, whatever be the propensities in future life. What are you to do with a young man up to the age of seventeen? Just as if . . . from the mere necessity of doing something, and the impossibility of doing any thing else, you were driven to the expedient of (Greek and Latin) metre and poetry;—as if a young man in that period might not acquire the modern languages, modern history, experimental philosophy, geography, chronology, and a considerable share of mathematics;—as if the memory of things were not more agreeable, and more profitable, than the memory of words.

from *The Edinburgh Review*, October, 1809

Female Education

As long as boys and girls run about in the dirt, and trundle hoops together, they are both precisely alike. If you catch up one half of these creatures, and train them to a particular set of actions and opinions, and the other half to a perfectly opposite set, of course their understandings will differ . . . It is not easy to imagine that there can be any just cause why a woman of forty should be more ignorant than a boy of twelve years of age . . . Now, there is a very general notion, that the moment you put the education of women upon a better footing than it is at present, at that moment there will be an end of all domestic economy; and that, if you once suffer women to eat of the tree of knowledge, the rest of the family will very soon be reduced to the same kind of aerial and unsatisfactory diet. (Yet) can any thing, for example, be more perfectly absurd than to suppose, that the care and perpetual solicitude which a mother feels for her children, depends upon her ignorance of Greek and Mathematics; and that she would desert an infant for a quadratic equation? . . . We are astonished, in hearing men converse on such subjects, to find them attributing such beautiful effects to ignorance. It would appear . . . that ignorance had been the great civilizer of the world. Women are delicate and refined, only because they are ignorant; they manage their household, only because they are ignorant; they attend to their children, only because they know no better.

. . . As the matter stands at present, half the talent in the universe runs to waste, and is totally unprofitable. It would have been almost as well for the world, hitherto, that women, instead of possessing the capacities they do at present, should have been born wholly destitute of wit, genius, and every other attribute of mind . . . If it can be shown that women may be trained to reason and imagine as well as men, the strongest reasons are necessary to show us why we should not avail ourselves of such rich gifts of nature. . . .

. . . Now, though it were denied that the acquisition of serious knowledge is of itself important to a woman, still it prevents a taste for silly and pernicious works of imagination;—it keeps away the horrid trash of novels. . . .

from The Edinburgh Review, January, 1810

An End of Term Report
(from the early nineteenth century)

The Mall, Chiswick, June 15, 18—.

Madam,—After her six years' residence at the Mall, I have the honour and happiness of presenting Miss Amelia Sedley to her parents, as a young lady not unworthy to occupy a fitting position in their polished and refined circle. Those virtues which characterize the young English gentlewoman, those accomplishments which become her birth and station, will not be found wanting in the amiable Miss Sedley, whose *industry* and *obedience* have endeared her to her instructors, and whose delightful sweetness of temper has charmed her *aged* and her *youthful* companions.

In music, in dancing, in orthography, in every variety of embroidery and needle-work, she will be found to have realized her friend's *fondest wishes*. In geography there is still much to be desired; and a careful and undeviating use of the backboard, for four hours daily during the next three years, is recommended as necessary to the acquirement of that dignified *deportment and carriage*, so requisite for every young lady of *fashion*.

In the principles of religion and morality, Miss Sedley will be found worthy of an establishment which has been honoured by the presence of *The Great Lexicographer* (Dr. Samuel Johnson), and the patronage of the admirable Mrs. Chapone. In leaving the Mall, Miss Amelia carries with her the hearts of her companions and the affectionate regards of her mistress, who has the honour to subscribe herself,

Madam,
Your most obliged humble servant,
BARBARA PINKERTON.

from *Vanity Fair*, 1847, by William Makepeace Thackeray

The Education of the Poor

To make society happy, and people easy, under the meanest circumstances, it is requisite that great numbers of them should be ignorant, as well as poor. Knowledge both enlarges and multiplies our desires; and the fewer things a man wishes for, the more easily his necessities may be supplied. The welfare and felicity of every state and kingdom, require, that the knowledge of the working poor should be confined within the verge of their occupations, and never extend (as to things visible) beyond what relates to their calling. The more a shepherd, a ploughman, or any other peasant, knows of the world, and the things that are foreign to his labour or employment, the less fit he'll be to go through the fatigues and hardships of it with cheerfulness and content.

from *Essay on Charity and Charity Schools*, c. 1805
by the Rev. Dr. Mandeville

Education and the Working Man

I am not one to sneer at education, but I would not give 6d in hiring an engineman because of his knowing how to read or write. I believe that of the two, the non-reading man is best. If you are going 5 or 6 miles without anything to attract your attention, depend upon it you will begin thinking of something else. It is impossible that a man who indulges in reading should make a good engine driver; it requires a species of machine, an intelligent man, a sober man, a steady man, but I would much rather not have a thinking man.

Isambard Kingdom Brunel, 1844

Present Times,
or Eight Shillings a Week

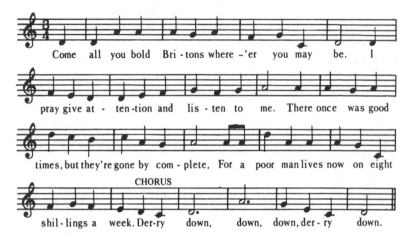

Come all you bold Bri-tons where-'er you may be. I
pray give at-ten-tion and lis-ten to me. There once was good
times, but they're gone by com-plete, For a poor man lives now on eight

CHORUS

shil-lings a week. Der-ry down, down, down, der-ry down.

Such times in old England there never was seen,
As the present ones now, but much better have been.
A poor man's condemned and considered a thief,
And compelled to work hard on eight shillings a week.

Our venerable fathers remember the year,
When a man earned three shillings a day and his beer.
He then could live well, keep his family neat,
But now he must work for eight shillings a week.

The Nobs of Old England, of shameful renown,
Are striving to crush a poor man to the ground.
They'll beat down their wages and starve them complete,
And make them work hard for eight shillings a week.

A poor man to labour, believe me 'tis so,
To maintain his family is willing to go
Either hedging or ditching, to plough or to reap,
But how does he live on eight shillings a week?

In the reign of old George, as you all understand,
Then there was contentment throughout the whole land.

Each poor man could live and get plenty to eat,
But now he must pine on eight shillings a week.

So now to conclude and finish my song,
May the times be much better before very long;
May every labourer be able to keep
His children and wife on twelve shillings a week.

Folk song of the 1830's

"A Contest between Futrell and Jackson" by James Gillray

The Fight

Reader, have you ever seen a fight? If not, you have a pleasure to come, at least if it is a fight like that between the Gas-man and Bill Neate. The crowd was very great when we arrived upon the spot; open carriages were coming up, with streamers flying and music playing, and the country-people were pouring in over hedge and ditch in all directions, to see their hero beat or be beaten. The odds were still on Gas, but only about five to four. Gully had been down to try Neate, and had backed him considerably, which was a damper to the sanguine confidence of the adverse party. About two hundred thousand pounds were pending . . . The day was fine for a December morning. The grass was wet, and the ground miry, and ploughed up with multitudinous feet, except that, within the ring itself, there was a spot of virgin-green closed in and unprofaned by vulgar tread, that shone with dazzling brightness in the mid-day sun. For it was now noon, and we had an hour to wait. This is the trying time. It is then the heart sickens, as you think what the two champions are about, and how short a time will determine their fate . . . The *swells* were parading in their white box-coats, the outer ring was cleared with some bruises on the heads and shins of the rustic assembly . . . ; the time drew near, I had got a good stand; a bustle, a buzz, ran through the crowd, and from the opposite side entered Neate, between his second and bottle-holder. He rolled along, swathed in his loose great coat, his knock-knees bending under his huge bulk; and, with a modest cheerful air, threw his hat into the ring. He then just looked round, and began quietly to undress; when from the other side there was a similar rush and an opening made, and the Gas-man came forward with a conscious air of anticipated triumph, too much like the cock-of-the-walk. He strutted about more than became a hero, sucked oranges with a supercilious air, and threw away the skin with a toss of his head, and went up and looked at Neate . . . The only sensible thing he did was, as he strode away from the modern Ajax, to fling out his arms, as if he wanted to try whether they would do their work that day. By this time they had stripped, and presented a strong contrast in appearance. If Neate was like Ajax, "with Atlantean shoulders, fit to bear" the pugilistic reputation of all Bristol, Hickman might be compared to Diomed, light, vigorous, elastic, and his back glistened in the sun, as he moved about, like a panther's hide. There was now a dead pause—attention was awe-struck. Who at that moment, big with a great event, did not draw his breath short—did not feel his heart throb? All was ready. They tossed up for the sun, and the Gas-man won. They were led up to the *scratch*—shook hands, and went at it.

In the first round every one thought it was all over. After making play a short time, the Gas-man flew at his adversary like a tiger, struck five blows in as many seconds, three first, and then following him as he staggered back, two more, right and left, and down he fell, a mighty ruin. There was a shout, and I said, "There is no standing this." Neate seemed like a lifeless lump of flesh and bone, round which the Gas-man's blows played with the rapidity of electricity or lightning, and you imagined he would only be lifted up to be knocked down again. It was as if Hickman held a sword or a fire in that right hand of his, and directed it against an unarmed body. They met again, and Neate seemed, not cowed, but particularly cautious. I saw his teeth clenched together and his brows knit close against the sun. He held out both his arms at full length straight before him, like two sledge-hammers, and raised his left an inch or two higher. The Gas-man could not get over this guard—they struck mutually and fell, but without advantage on either side. It was the same in the next round; but the balance of power was thus restored—the fate of the battle was suspended. No one could tell how it would end. This was the only moment in which opinion was divided; for, in the next, the Gas-man aiming a mortal blow at his adversary's neck with his right hand, and failing from the length he had to reach, the other returned it with his left at full swing, planted a tremendous blow on his cheek-bone and eyebrow, and made a red ruin of that side of his face. The Gas-man went down, and there was another shout—a roar of triumph as the waves of fortune rolled tumultuously from side to side. This was a settler.

Hickman got up, and "grinned horrible a ghastly smile", yet he was evidently dashed in his opinion of himself; it was the first time he had ever been so punished; all one side of his face was perfect scarlet, and his right eye was closed in dingy blackness, as he advanced to the fight, less confident, but still determined. After one or two rounds,

35

not receiving another such remembrancer, he rallied and went at it with his former impetuousity. But in vain. His strength had been weakened,—his blows could not tell at such a distance,—he was obliged to fling himself at his adversary, and could not strike from his feet; and almost as regularly as he flew at him with his right hand, Neate warded the blow, or drew back out of its reach, and felled him with the return of his left. . . From this time forward the event became more certain every round; and about the twelfth it seemed as if it must have been over. Hickman generally stood with his back to me; but in the scuffle, he had changed positions, and Neate just then made a tremendous lunge at him, and hit him full in the face. It was doubtful whether he would fall backwards or forwards; he hung suspended for a second or two, and then fell back, throwing his hands in the air, and with his face lifted up to the sky. I never saw any thing more terrific than his aspect just before he fell. All traces of life, of natural expression, were gone from him. His face was like a human skull, a death's head, spouting blood. The eyes were filled with blood, the nose streamed with blood, the mouth gaped blood . . . Yet he fought on after this for several rounds, still striking the first desperate blow, and Neate standing on the defensive, and using the same cautious guard to the last, as if he had still all his work to do; and it was not till the Gas-man was so stunned in the seventeenth or eighteenth round, that his senses forsook him, and he could not come to time, that the battle was declared over . . . When the Gas-man came to himself, the first words he uttered were, "Where am I? What is the matter?" "Nothing is the matter, Tom,—you have lost the battle, but you are the bravest man alive." And Jackson whispered to him, "I am collecting a purse for you, Tom."

from *The Fight*, 1822, by William Hazlitt

Dangerous Sports

It is not necessary to mount a horse to be exposed to danger from him since several children have had their skulls beat to pieces from the kick of a horse, in consequence of their sillily plucking the hairs of its tail. Indeed of such different tempers are these animals that he must be more bold than prudent who ventures within reach of their heels. So ferocious are they sometimes, that two dreadful instances have occurred lately; in one of which the hand of a gentleman was seized by a horse and terribly ground by his teeth. In the other, an enraged horse seized the arm of a poor man which he did not loosen until the bystanders had broken the bone of his nose by beating him; and the arm was so injured as to be obliged to be cut off.

*   *   *

Never stand opposite to anyone who is spinning his top, nor sufficiently near to his side to receive it on your head should it hang in the string.

*   *   *

Think before you taste, and taste before you swallow. For want of attending to this simple rule I knew two poor children lose their lives. One from thoughtlessly tasting something he found in a bottle, which was aqua fortis and had his mouth and throat so burnt that he died in the greatest agonies. The other was a little girl, who playing alone in a parlour, perceived a bottle of liquor standing on the sideboard. On tasting the liquor she found it pleasant, and putting her mouth to the bottle drank so freely that when her mother came into the room she found her senseless on the floor. The liquor she had drunk was brandy, and in a very few hours she died.

*   *   *

Very lately a most dreadful accident happened in the country. The guards of the mail coaches always travel with loaded pistols and a blunderbuss. In a room at an inn, some of the pistols had been left by one of the guards, and had remained there several days when a little boy about eleven years of age took up one of the pistols and

37

carried it into the garden as a plaything. On his return to the house he met his sister, towards whom he presented the pistol and snapped it several times. At last most unexpectedly and unfortunately it went off and its whole contents were lodged in her stomach: she survived only a few hours during which she suffered the most excruciating torments.

from *Dangerous Sports*, 1808, by James Parkinson

"Bull-Baiting" by Thomas Rowlandson

The Liverpool Grand National Steeplechase, 1839. (Note the lead horses' "flying gallop"—an impossible posture which was not disproved until the use of photography later in the century)

Cricket

Three good strong sticks of about two feet in length are driven into the ground at about four inches asunder. In the top of each is cut a little notch, and a small piece of wood is laid across from one to the other. The upright sticks are distinguished by the name of *stumps*; the cross one by that of the *bail*. This wicket—for that is the name by which it is called—is placed about the middle of the field. The players divide themselves into two parties, and toss up, as in many other games, for the first innings. One party, who is out, bowls the ball from the distance of about thirty yards, towards the wicket, which it is the business of the *bat's man* to defend. If he is fortunate enough to give it a good stroke he immediately sets off to run as far as the line at thirty yards distance, where the opposite party stood when they bowled; and if he can touch it with his bat and get home to the wicket before one of the adverse party has knocked off the bail with the ball, he reckons one. If the ball has been struck to such a distance that he thinks he shall have time for a second run, he may go on again, and reckon as many notches as he takes runs to the appointed place and back again during the time that he remained *in*, but if his adversary strike off the bail either in bowling, or while he is running, or catch the ball when he had struck it and before it touched the ground he is *out*, and is obliged to resign the bat to one of his own party, till they each have their innings; and then the opposite party come in.

The bat's man is the only *player* of the party that is *in*, who is engaged, but all of the other party are employed—one in bowling, the others in trying to stop or catch the ball when struck, and endeavouring to knock off the bail with the ball while the bat's man is running, and those who are thus engaged are called the *seekers-out*. When all the players have had two innings, the game is finished, and that party is winner which has gained most notches.

from The Book of Games; or, a History of Juvenile Sports
practised at a considerable Academy near London, 1812

"Mr Hope of Amsterdam Playing Cricket with his Friends", 1792, by J. Sablet

"The Shipwreck" by J. M. W. Turner

New Ways of Seeing

The sea up to that time had been generally regarded by painters as a liquidly composed, level-seeking consistent thing, with a smooth surface, rising to a water-mark on sides of ships; in which ships were scientifically to be embedded, and wetted, up to said water-mark, and to remain dry above the same. But Turner found during his Southern Coast tour that the sea was *not* this: that it was, on the contrary, a very incalculable and unhorizontal thing, setting its "water-mark" sometimes on the highest heavens, as well as on sides of ships;—very breakable into pieces; half of a wave separable from the other half, and on the instant carriageable miles inland;—not in any wise limiting itself to a state of apparent liquidity, but now striking like a steel gauntlet, and now becoming a cloud, and vanishing, no eye can tell whither; one moment a flint cave, the next a marble pillar, the next a mere white fleece thickening the thundery rain. He never forgot those facts; never afterwards was able to recover the idea of positive distinction between sea and sky, or sea and land. Steel gauntlet, black rock, white cloud, and men and masts, gnashed to pieces and disappearing in a few breaths and splinters among them;—a little blood on the rock angle, like red sea-weed, sponged away by the next splash of the foam, and the glistering granite and green water all pure again in vacant wrath. So stayed by him, for ever, the Image of the Sea.

from *Turner*, 1836, by John Ruskin

Scenerymania

The scenery is very wild and picturesque to Aberfoyle. We left Mr. Bewick to sketch at the little inn, and the rest of us went on to the manse, where we saw Francis, as stout and taller than he was, the Doctor and Mrs. Graham, his son and daughter, a stranger lady and another boarder, besides young Glen, so their pastoral abode seemed pretty well filled. At the manse the scene improves in beauty and Mama promised the Doctor to come back and take a proper view of it afterwards. We took Francis along with us, as Mr. Graham had asked him to dine at Gartmore.

We then proceeded to Loch Ard. The road all the way is beautiful, sometimes enclosed with high woody banks and natural birch waving their graceful leaves over it, sometimes by the side of the loch, which was smooth as glass without a wave, and the other side steep rocks covered with purple heath, foxglove, the bright green fern, the wild honeysuckle, myrtle, and moss of many various kinds. . . . There were different opinions sported when we arrived at the margin of the lake. Mama said she would like to live here for the summer and go out every day, stay out all day either sketching or boating or clambering up these rocks and beautiful glens. Mr. Napier shrugged his shoulders, and said he should think himself in a very pitiable situation in such. It became every instant more beautiful till we stopped at the inn, if so it can be called, where Mr. Bewick and Mama took out their pencils. Francis longed for a fishing rod, Papa sauntered about, and Mr. Napier, Miss Bogle and I went up the glen which commanded a beautiful view of the lake, and which ought to be called the Glen of Green Caterpillars, for our bonnets and shawls were covered with them when we came down. After resting here a considerable time, it was agreed that it would not be fitting to keep the laird's dinner waiting so we set out again on our return. . . .

At dinner everyone was full of what they had seen and nothing else was talked of. Everyone was "scenery mad". "Scenerymania" was the order of the day, even Mr. Napier laid aside his dogs and coursing and birds to tell how very beautiful it was, the view from the glen above the inn particularly. He went away after dinner to Ballikinrain. I had more opportunity this evening of seeing what kind of a person Miss Beatson, the governess, was. I was much struck with the peculiar cast of her countenance and thought she must be somewhat of an oddity. She is exceedingly romantic, writes poetry, some pieces of which I saw, and seems not to falsify my idea of her from her looks, which are plain but singular.

from the diary of Helen Graham (entry for 15th June, 1825)

Roads

The turnpike roads in Middlesex bear evident marks of their vicinity to a great city. Scattered villas and genteel houses, in the manner of a continued and rather elegant village, are erected on one or both sides of the roads, for three, five, or seven miles out of London. The footpaths are thronged with passengers, and the carriage-ways with horses, carts, waggons, chaises, and gentlemen's carriages of every description.

This country is intersected by the three most frequented turn-pike roads in the kingdom, namely, the great western road, the great north road, and the eastern, or Harwich road; as also by many others of less note.

Most of the parish highways in the country are superior to any other of equal extent that I have ever seen. They are hard and clean in every sort of weather; so much so, that gentlemen may ride along them, even directly after rain, and scarcely receive a splash.

The turnpike roads, on the contrary, are generally very bad; although at the toll-gates of this county there is collected a very large sum of money, probably not less than £30,000 a year, which is uselessly expended in sinking wells, erecting pumps, building carts, and hiring horses and men, to keep the dust down by watering, instead of more wisely scraping it off. By the folly of this practice, the roads are kept many inches deep in mud. The mud indeed is so very deep all the winter, and so fluid after rain, as to render it unsafe to meet horses, owing to their feet throwing the mud not only over a horseman's clothes but also into his eyes.

The road from Tyburn through Uxbridge is supposed to have more broad-wheeled waggons pass over it than any other in the county. During the whole of the winter 1797–8 there was but one passable track on this road, and that was less than six feet wide, and was eight inches deep in fluid mud. All the rest of the road was a foot to eighteen inches deep in adhesive mud. This track was thronged with waggons (many of them drawn by ten horses, and most of them having broad wheels, even to sixteen inches wide) and farmers' six-inch-wheel carts, which occupied almost the whole of this confined space. It was therefore with great difficulty, and some danger, that horsemen and light carriages could pass.

The road from Hyde-park-corner through Brentford and Hounslow is equally deep in filth. Notwithstanding His Majesty travels this road several times every week, there are not any exertions made towards keeping it clean in winter.

from *View of the Agriculture of Middlesex*, 1798, by John Middleton

"The Mail Coach in a Flood" by James Pollard

New Form of Travel

To-day we have had a *lark* of a very high order. Lady Wilton sent over yesterday from Knowsley to say that the Loco Motive machine was to be upon the railway at such a place at 12 o'clock for the Knowsley party to ride in if they liked, and inviting this house to be of the party. So of course we were at our post in 3 carriages and some horsemen at the hour appointed. I had the satisfaction, for I can't call it *pleasure*, of taking a trip of five miles in it, which we did in just a quarter of an hour—that is, 20 miles an hour. As accuracy upon this subject was my great object, I held my watch in my hand at starting, and all the time; and as it has a second hand, I knew I could not be deceived; and it so turned out there was not the difference of a second between the coachee or conductor and myself. But observe, during these five miles, the machine was occasionally made to put itself out or *go it*; and then we went at the rate of 23 miles an hour, and just with the same ease as to motion or absence of friction as the other reduced pace. But the quickest motion is to me *frightful*: it is really flying, and it is impossible to divest yourself of the notion of instant death to all upon the least accident happening. It gave me a headache which has not left me yet. Sefton is convinced that some damnable thing must come of it; but he and I seem more struck with such apprehension than others. . . . The smoke is very inconsiderable indeed, but sparks of fire are abroad in some quantity: one burnt Miss de Ros's cheek, another a hole in Lady Maria's silk pelisse, and a third a hole in some one else's gown. Altogether I am extremely glad indeed to have seen this miracle, and to have travelled in it. Had I thought worse of it than I do, I should have had the curiosity to try it; but, having done so, I am quite satisfied with my *first* achievement being my *last*.

from a letter by Thomas Creevey to Miss Ord, 14th November, 1829

Barton aqueduct carrying the Bridgewater canal over the river Irwell

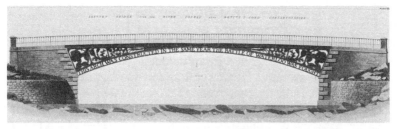

Llynnon bridge over the river Conway, designed by Thomas Telford, 1815

Excavation of Olive Mount, near Liverpool, 1831

The First Balloon Flight
and Parachute Drop over Britain

[Vincenti Lunardi] assended in a Boolone [15th September, 1784] at the artillry ground [Finsbury] London to a great Hithe over Barnat, North Hall, then went for St Albans, then took his course East over Codicot, Wellwin, Tewin, Bengeo & Landed him self in a Little Meadow at Standon Green End, he throwd his line out & was pulled Down by a young woman in the meadow, who was fritned at first & Run away, thought it the Devell, till he made her sencable & gave her 5 guineas, it was a very fine hot day, I saw him plane as he came over Bacons, he was at a Great Hight for his Boloon was 30 feet round but apeard no biger than a Boys Kite, maney people followed him on Hors back & foot & was up soon after he fell, & Wm Baker Esqr of Bayford Bury took him home in his Carriage to the Bury & his Boloon & was their some time, a weak or more, & Baker had a great pipble stone which had lane in Bengeo street as no one knows how long remoovd to the place he fell & a Brass plate put theiron with the Account, I suppose the stone to way 3 Hund, people used to sit on it in the street as it was by the path side.

*　　　*　　　*

[1802] On tuesday the 21 acended in a Bloon at London Garmeran [Louis Garnerin] about 5000 feet High & their cut with his Knife the Strings that fastened his carr that he sat in from the bloon & cam down to the Earth with a Parashute over his head unhert, to save his fall.

from the *Diary and Reminiscences* of John Carrington, 1726–1810

A Medical Controversy
Cowpox Vaccination versus Smallpox Inoculation

The security derived from vaccination, if not absolutely perfect, is as nearly so as can perhaps be expected from any human discovery; for, amongst several hundred thousand cases, with the results of which the College have been made acquainted, the number of alleged failures has been surprisingly small; so much so, as to form certainly no reasonable objection to the general adoption of vaccination; for it appears, that there are not nearly so many failures in a given number of vaccinated persons, as there are deaths in an equal number of persons inoculated for the smallpox.

from *Report of the Royal College of Physicians on Vaccination*, 8th July, 1807

£30,000 for the Cow-Pox ! ! ! An address (to Lord H.P. and) to the British Parliament on Vaccination (of the greatest Importance to Mankind); wherein the Report of the College of Physicians is completely confuted.

. . . Celebrated and illustrious senators of Britain, lay aside all prejudice, and receive, I entreat you, the following information with candour and attention, viz. that all the physicians, surgeons and apothecaries, most eminently distinguished for abilities and professional skill, *all to a man,* now acknowledge, that vaccination is not a certain preventive of the smallpox; and that it sometimes produces new, dangerous, and fatal diseases. These *truths* are at this time universally granted, and candidly acknowledged by every intelligent medical gentleman. . . .

The *Omnipotent* GOD of *Nature,* the inconceivable *Creator of all existence,* has permitted *Evil, Buonoparte,* and *Vaccination* to exist,—to prosper—and even to triumph for a short space of time,—perhaps as the scourge and punishment of mankind for their sins, and for reasons no doubt the best--But, are we to worship—to applaud—or even to submit to *Evil,* to *Buonoparte,*—or to *Vaccination,*—because they have for some time been prosperous ?—No!

Among the numerous shocking cases of cowpox which I have heard of, I know not if the most horrible of all has yet been published, viz. of a child at Peckham, who, after being inoculated with the cowpox, had its former natural disposition absolutely changed to the *brutal,* so that it ran upon all fours like a BEAST, bellowing like a cow, and butting with its head like a bull. For my part, I can scarcely think it possible, having had no time to ascertain the truth.

Ferdinand Smyth Stuart, 1807

"The Cow-Pock—or—The Wonderful Effects of the New Inoculation!"
by James Gillray (Dr Edward Jenner tests his new vaccine
with dramatic results)

A Letter to Sir Humphry Davy

1st June, 1816

After having introduced your safety-lamp into general use in all
the collieries under my direction, where inflammable air prevails,
and after using them daily in every variety of explosive mixture for
upwards of three months, I feel the highest possible gratification
in stating to you that they have answered to my entire satisfaction.

The safety of the lamps is so easily proved by taking them into
any part of a mine charged with fire-damp, and all the explosive
gradations of that dangerous element are so easily and satisfactorily
ascertained by their application, as to strike the minds of the most
prejudiced with the strongest conviction of their high utility;
and our colliers have adopted them with the greatest eagerness.

Besides the facilities afforded by this invention to the working of
coal mines abounding in fire-damp, it has enabled the directors

and superintendents to ascertain, with the utmost precision and expedition, both the presence, the quantity, and the correct situation of the gas. Instead of creeping inch by inch with a candle, as is usual, along the galleries of a mine suspected to contain fire-damp, in order to ascertain its presence, we walk firmly in with the safe-lamps, and with the utmost confidence prove the actual state of the mine. By observing attentively the several appearances upon the flame of the lamp, in an examination of this kind, the cause of accidents, which have happened to the most experienced and cautious miners, is completely developed; and this has been, in a great measure, matter of mere conjecture.

I feel peculiar satisfaction in dwelling upon a subject which is of the utmost importance, not only to the great cause of humanity, and to the mining interest of the country, but also to the commercial and manufacturing interests of the United Kingdom; for I am convinced that by the happy invention of the safe-lamp, large proportions of the coal mines of the empire will be rendered available, which otherwise might have remained inaccessible—at least without an invention of similar utility, it could not have been wrought without much loss of the mineral, and risk of life and capital.

It is not necessary that I should enlarge upon the national advantages which must necessarily result from an invention calculated to prolong our supply of mineral coal, because I think them obvious to every reflecting mind; but I cannot conclude without expressing my highest sentiments of admiration for those talents which have developed the properties, and controlled the power, of one of the most dangerous elements which human enterprize has hitherto had to encounter.

John Buddle

"A Pit Head" *c.* 1820 (showing steam winding gear)

Great Britain is the Noblest Land

Great Bri-tain is the no - blest land That e'er the world could boast When free-dom re - gu-lates com - mands, And her we love the most, And her we love the most.

CHORUS

The King, the Na-tion, and the Law, We're hap-py to o - bey Then Vive le Roi, Vive le Roi, and Vive la li - ber-té! The King, the Na-tion,

and the Law, We're hap-py to o - bey___ Then
Vive le Roi, Vive le Roi, and Vive la li - ber - té!

The birds unshackled rove the air,
The fishes swim the seas,
No fetters e'er could Britons bear,
Then why, my boys, should we?
Then why, my boys, should we?

Tho' all the base in arms should rise
To rob us of our goods,
Yet ev'ry effort we'd despise,
Their rage should be withstood,
Their rage should be withstood.

from the opera, *The Picture of Paris*, 1790

The Mechanical Age

Were we required to characterize this age of ours by any single epithet, we should be tempted to call it, not an Heroical, Devotional, Philosophical, or Moral Age, but, above all others, the Mechanical Age. It is the Age of Machinery, in every outward and inward sense of that word; the age which, with its whole undivided might, forwards, teaches, and practises the great art of adapting means to ends. Nothing is now done directly, or by hand; all is by rule and calculated contrivance. For the simplest operation, some helps and accompaniments, some cunning abbreviating process is in readiness. Our old modes of exertion are all discredited, and thrown aside. On every hand, the living artisan is driven from his workshop, to make room for a speedier, inanimate one. The shuttle drops from the fingers of the weaver, and falls into iron fingers that ply it faster.

The sailor furls his sail, and lays down his oar; and bids a strong, unwearied servant, on vaporous wings, bear him through the waters. Men have crossed oceans by steam; the Birmingham Fire-king has visited the fabulous East; . . . There is no end to machinery. Even the horse is stripped of his harness, and finds a fleet fire-horse yoked in his stead. Nay, we have an artist that hatches chickens by steam; the very brood-hen is to be superseded! For all earthly, and for some unearthly purposes, we have machines and mechanic furtherances; for mincing our cabbages; for casting us into magnetic sleep. We remove mountains, and make seas our smooth highway; nothing can resist us. We war with rude Nature; and, by our resist-less engines, come off always victorious, and loaded with spoils.

What wonderful accessions have thus been made, and are still making, to the physical power of mankind; how much better fed, clothed, lodged and, in all outward respects, accommodated men now are, or might be, by a given quantity of labour, is a grateful reflection which forces itself on every one. What changes, too, this addition of power is introducing into the Social System; how wealth has more and more increased, and at the same time gathered itself more and more into masses, strangely altering the old relations, and increasing the distance between the rich and the poor, will be a question for Political Economists, and a much more complex and important one than any they have yet engaged with.

from *Signs of the Times*, 1829, by Thomas Carlyle

Conversation

"How do you live upon half a crown a week?"

"I don't live upon it," said he.

"How do you live then?"

"Why," said he, "I poach, it is better to be hanged than to be starved to death."

conversation between William Cobbett and a poacher, recorded in the *Political Register*, 29th March, 1823

"Execution at Newgate" by Thomas Rowlandson

Two "Irish" Cases

UNION-HALL

Wednesday.—Patrick Daley, Timothy Sullivan, Thomas Sullivan, Thomas Daley, Patrick Roche, John Sullivan, Bridget Daley, and Julia Azell, all Irish, were brought up in custody, charged with a riot and assault, and with having wounded a patrol, named Holt, whose recovery is very doubtful. The prisoners, when placed at the bar, exhibited a disgusting and frightful appearance, being covered with blood.—James Hill, a patrol of Clink Liberty, stated, that on Tuesday night, about 12 o'clock, some of the prisoners passed him on his beat, and went into a house in Paver's-alley, Lomas's-fields; they appeared to be intoxicated. Some little time after he heard the cries of murder proceed from the house into which the prisoners went. Witness went to the door of the house, which was shut. On demanding admittance, a voice cried out from within—"If you come here, you'll be murdered; we have a pitchfork ready for you."

Witness replied, "I have a pistol for you," and instantly sprung his rattle for assistance. He was soon joined by a number of patrol and watchmen, with whose assistance he broke open a window, through which they dragged out J. Sullivan, who guarded the window inside, and made a desperate resistance. Having taken him to the watch-house, witness returned, and Timothy Sullivan, who had succeeded his namesake as guard on the window, was dragged out and lodged in the watch-house. On returning to the house, witness heard a noise, as if the rioters were breaking into the adjoining house, and for the purpose of preventing their escape he went into the next house, where he found P. Daley, near naked and covered with blood, who was also secured and taken to the watch-house. The witness produced the butt-ends of two horse pistols, with marks of blood on them, which belonged to pistols taken from Holt the patrol, who had entered the house during the witness's absence with the prisoners he took to the watch-house; witness also produced a hammer with blood on it. John McDonald, a patrol, who had his head bound up in consequence of the brutal treatment he received, stated, that on hearing the rattle he ran to the scene of action. Holt (who now lies at the hospital) and the witness assisted in breaking open the window. Holt put in one leg, and was instantly dragged into the room. Witness put his head in, and received a blow of a poker, which knocked him into the street, where he lay insensible for some time. On recovering himself, he saw the first witness and another patrol dragging the prisoner, 'Pat.' Daley, through the window. Witness identified Daley as the man who struck him; witness assisted in taking him to the watch-house, and on his return, saw Holt lying on the floor of the room, and the prisoner, Thomas Daley, standing over him with a hammer in his hand, with which he beat Holt on different parts of the body; the butt-ends of the pistols lay close by on the floor. Holt was covered with blood, and quite insensible. The riot lasted two hours. John Wilson, another patrol, corroborated the former witness's evidence, and stated, that on attempting to enter the house, he was struck with a poker, and had the bridge of his nose broken. One of the prisoners had a pistol in his hand, and Bridget Daley had a fender, with which she stood near the window, making thrusts at everyone that attempted to enter. Mr. Kenrick, a baker, residing in Union-street, on hearing the cries of murder, went to the house from which the cries proceeded, and saw McDonald knocked down by one of the prisoners. Witness instantly seized the cutlass and pistol from one of the patrol, and jumped into the room through the window. John Sullivan was standing in the middle of the room with a pistol in his hand, swearing that he would be the death of the first man that offered to touch him. Witness instantly snapped the pistol at him, but it missed fire several times. Witness then cut him down with the sword, and secured Pat. Daley, who defended himself with a chair, and defied the witness to fire. The witness identified all the prisoners as having been present. Mr. Morris, an assistant in St. Thomas's Hospital, attended, and stated that Holt, the patrol, had received a severe wound on the head, and had several contusions on the body. He did not consider him in immediate danger, but danger might come on. The Magistrate requested that a certificate might be sent from the hospital signifying the state of the patrol tomorrow, and remanded the prisoners for another examination, observing at the same time, that he had never heard of a more cowardly and disgraceful attack upon a man who lay insensible on the floor.

TOWN HALL

John Barry, an Irishman, was charged by the landlord of a public house in Tooley-street, because he kicked up some row in his tap-room. The publican said he "only wanted to get rid of him"; but Pat would not be so got rid of, and the following facts came out:— On Tuesday, Paddy, whilst sauntering for work, met a seaman, who employed him to carry a heavy burden to the complainant's house, for which he gave him 6d. and a pint of beer, and hired him again to go the Bricklayer's Arms to bring more luggage, and on this occasion he was to be remunerated with a shilling. The job was performed, the sailor changed a sovereign and paid his way, leaving Paddy's "thirteener" with the landlady; this LADY told the man that 6d. only had been left for him, but Pat suspecting a bit of a "chouse", "kicked up a bobbery", and he was sent to the watch-house. The Magistrate said, if the shilling was left at the bar, it was shameful to keep it from a poor fellow out of work. He hoped the trifle would be paid, and that it would not be necessary for him to say any more on the subject. The prisoner was discharged, and as he left the office said "Well, by the powers, did any one ever see such chape, aisy law, and such a jontleman too—no trouble at all with him?" The poor simple fellow thinking his night's imprisonment no inconvenience or trouble whatever.

from the first issue of *The Sunday Times*, 20th October, 1822

The Dungeon

And this place our forefathers made for man!
This is the process of our love and wisdom,
To each poor brother who offends against us—
Most innocent, perhaps—and what if guilty?
Is this the only cure? Merciful God?
Each pore and natural outlet shrivell'd up
By ignorance and parching poverty,
His energies roll back upon his heart,
And stagnate and corrupt; till changed to poison,
They break out on him, like a loathsome plague-spot;
Then we call in our pamper'd mountebanks—
And this is their best cure! uncomforted
And friendless solitude, groaning and tears,
And savage faces, at the clanking hour,
Seen through the steams and vapour of his dungeon,
By the lamp's dismal twilight! So he lies
Circled with evil, till his very soul
Unmoulds its essence, hopelessly deformed
By sights of ever more deformity!

With other ministrations thou, O nature!
Healest thy wandering and distempered child:
Thou pourest on him thy soft influences,
Thy sunny hues, fair forms, and breathing sweets,
Thy melodies of woods, and winds, and waters,
Till he relent, and can no more endure
To be a jarring and a dissonant thing,

Amid this general dance and minstrelsy;
But bursting into tears, wins back his way,
His angry spirit healed and harmonized
By the benignant touch of love and beauty.

from *Lyrical Ballads*, 1798, by William Wordsworth

The Press Gang

"I say, gentlemen, the liberty of the subject cannot be violated!
I say that—thanks to the blessings of Magna Charta! the liberty of
an Englishman is inviolable! Neither Kings, Lords, nor Commons,
can lay a finger upon an Englishman if—"

Jack had not breath to finish the sentence, for a huge hand grasped
him by the collar, and a voice, harsh and deep as if the speaker had
availed himself of a trumpet, exclaimed—"Messmate, we want
you."

Jack Runnymede, convinced of the inviolability of the person of
an Englishman, indignantly screwed himself round, when he beheld
a man in a hairy cap and rough coat, not too closely buttoned to hide
a cutlass and a pair of pistols. The man, however, was not in a
sanguinary mood, as he held in his right hand nothing more than a
short, knotted cudgel no thicker than his arm. Besides, he was
evidently a good-tempered person if not too much put upon; for he
met the burning glances of Runnymede with a smile and a nod, and
the heartiest assurance that "he would be nicely provided for." "My
good men," said Runnymede, "you mistake the person—you do,
indeed." "Mistake! I ax your pardon—we've been arter you this
week," said the leader in the hairy cap.

*   *   *

"Stay—stay—one minute. Am I—" Jack was in agony as he put
what he felt to be a vital question—"am I to understand that you
wish to press me?—that you wish to drag me from my home?—
my—"

"Why, you know your wife's tired of you," cried the hairy cap,
"you know she is. Bring him along, lads."

59

"All I ask is this. Do you intend to use violence?—do you intend to press me for the fleet?" roared Runnymede.

"And nothing less, by—" The single oath was lost in the clamorous assent of the whole gang, who, like a pack of hounds, hung about the free-born Briton, yelling, cursing, screaming, fighting.

Jack fought desperately. A hundred times he wished for a sword, a pistol, a poker, any deadly weapon. "The law—thank God!—the law was on his side, and he might with impunity murder any number of his assailants."

"What a smart hand he'll make in a boarding party!"—was the derisive eulogy of one of the gang, as Jack, having seized a bludgeon from one of his enemies, cleared a circle about him, and then retreated with his back to a wall. Flourishing his cudgel around him, Jack Runnymede, like a gallant Briton, roared, at the pitch of his voice, "Remember, I warn you—it's illegal—against the law—in violation of—of—dearest rights—Englishmen—fellow countrymen—succour—it's your cause—yours as well as mine—Britons, your rights—your—"

Strange as it may appear to the reader, Jack Runnymede, calling upon the dearest hopes of his countrymen—appealing to them by their most sacred rights—by their love of their homes, their spouses, and their babes,—was suffered by staring Englishmen to be carried, like a carcase, away—not one British finger moving in his defence. Jack had been seized in the Minories; hence, only a short time elapsed ere he was safely stored in the Tower Tender. . . .

Jack, touched by the intense agony of one man, forgot the acuteness of his own suffering. The poor fellow was gathered in a ball in one corner—his trembling hands covered his face; tears trickled through his fingers; and his whole body heaved and quivered, as if he struggled with some burning poison. He fought against his grief, and yet, at intervals, he could not master it—it would burst forth in querulous moaning. . . .

"Don't despair, my good fellow," said Runnymede in a low voice, and after a long pause, to the disconsolate seaman. "I tell you there's a remedy—"

"Remedy! what remedy? Ar'n't we all here, like stolen niggers?—Hav'n't I lost my wife—my child? torn from 'em, for what I know, never to see their blessed eyes again?"

"Yes—very true—you are dragged from your home—as you say, from your wife and child—but still you may thank God"—

"For what?" roared the wretched husband and father.

"Why, that it's against Magna Charta—that it's a violation of the law—and that, in short, though treated like a beast, you are an Englishman."

Next morning, a vessel sailed for the Nore with Jack and his companions, the number being augmented by some half-dozen captives made by the gang in the course of the night. To all not utterly inconsolable, Runnymede dwelt upon the legal remedy for the abuse under which they suffered.

"And how, my good friend—how was it that you fell into their hands?" asked Jack of a melancholy newcomer.

"I was torn from my bed," answered the man, "the gang had heard that I had been to sea—they got in at the window—and—"

"And didn't you resist?" inquired Runnymede.

"I maimed one of 'em, I think—but 'twas no use; I was hauled off—my wife screaming—the children, in their bedclothes, crying—my old mother kneeling and cursing the gang,—and—there, mate, don't talk of it," and the man trembled from head to foot.

"Got into your house!" exclaimed Runnymede, "took you from your bed? Why, my dear friend, they can't do it."

"What do you mean by 'they can't do it'?" asked the man, with a scowl.

"Why, it's against the law; in open violation of that great principle which admits the meanest hut of the humblest Englishman to be his castle. I tell you again, my good friend, they can't do it."

"Well, if they can't do it, then I'm not here; so if you can persuade me to that, messmate—if you can make me believe that I'm now at home at breakfast, with my—there, let's have no more of it," cried the poor fellow, choking with emotion.

... The further adventures of Runnymede are no less improving, needless to say he was kept on board and introduced to a seaman's life, finally rising to purser and, with industry, retiring with a fortune. During his seafaring experiences, his views upon impressment had undergone a remarkable change. "Pray, sir," said he to a parliamentary candidate who solicited his support, "what are your views on impressment?"

"I am opposed most assuredly to the infamous and inhuman system of pressing," was the reply.

"My service to you, sir," said Jack Runnymede, "you don't have my vote—sweep us from the world as a naval power by doing away with impressment!—No, sir, not while I can lift my voice, will I consent to this. By losing this I should cease to be grateful, as I am, for my country—should no longer bless my stars that I am a Briton—no longer thank God that I am an Englishman."

from *Jack Runnymede* by Douglas Jerrold

Of the Division of Labour

The greatest improvement in the productive powers of labour, and the greater part of the skill, dexterity, and judgment with which it is any where directed, or applied, seem to have been the effects of the division of labour.

The effects of the division of labour, in the general business of society, will be more easily understood, by considering in what manner it operates in some particular manufactures. It is commonly supposed to be carried furthest in some very trifling ones; not perhaps that it really is carried further in them than in others of more importance: but in those trifling manufactures which are destined to supply the small wants of but a small number of people, the whole number of workmen must necessarily be small; and those employed in every different branch of the work can often be collected into the same workhouse, and placed at once under the view of the spectator. In those great manufactures, on the contrary, which are destined to supply the great wants of the great body of the people, every different branch of the work employs so great a number of workmen, that it is impossible to collect them all into the same workhouse. We can seldom see more, at one time, than those employed in one single branch. Though in such manufactures, therefore, the work may really be divided into a much greater number of parts, than in those of a more trifling nature, the division is not near so obvious, and has accordingly been much less observed.

To take an example, therefore, from a very trifling manufacture;

but one in which the division of labour has been very often taken notice of, the trade of the pinmaker; a workman not educated to this business (which the division of labour has rendered a distinct trade), nor acquainted with the use of the machinery employed in it (to the invention of which the same division of labour has probably given occasion), could scarce, perhaps, with the utmost industry, make one pin in a day, and certainly could not make twenty. But in the way in which the business is now carried on, not only the whole work is a peculiar trade, but it is divided into a number of branches, of which the greater part are likewise peculiar trades. One man draws out the wire, another straights it, a third cuts it, a fourth points it, a fifth grinds it at the top for receiving the head; to make the head requires two or three distinct operations; to put it on, is a peculiar business, to whiten the pins is another; it is even a trade by itself to put them into the paper; and the important business of making a pin is, in this manner, divided into about eighteen distinct operations, which, in some manufactories, are all performed by distinct hands, though in others the same man will sometimes perform two or three of them. I have seen a small manufactory of this kind where ten men only were employed, and where some of them consequently performed two or three distinct operations. But though they were very poor, and therefore but indifferently accommodated with the necessary machinery, they could, when they exerted themselves, make among them about twelve pounds of pins in a day. There are in a pound upwards of four thousand pins of a middling size. Those ten persons, therefore, could make among them upwards of forty-eight thousand pins in a day. Each person, therefore, making a tenth part of forty-eight thousand pins, might be considered as making four thousand eight hundred pins in a day. But if they had all wrought separately and independently, and without any of them having been educated to this peculiar business, they certainly could not each of them have made twenty, perhaps not one pin in a day; that is, certainly, not the two hundred and fortieth, perhaps not the four thousand eight hundredth part of what they are at present capable of performing, in consequence of a proper division and combination of their different operations.

from *The Wealth of Nations*, 1776, by Adam Smith

Working Conditions
The Framework Knitter

It was by a number of petty and vexatious grindings, in addition to the obnoxious "frame rent" (the worker had to pay rent for the machine at which he worked), that the poor framework knitter was worn down, till you might have known him by his peculiar air of misery and dejection, if you had met him a hundred miles from Leicester. He had to pay, not only "frame rent", but so much per week for the "standing" of the frame in the shop of the "master", for the frames were grouped together in the shops, generally, though you would often find a single frame in a weaver's cottage. The man had also to pay threepence per dozen to the "master" for "giving out" of the work. He had also to pay so much per dozen to the female "seamer" of the hose. And he had also oil to buy for his machine, and lights to pay for in the darker half of the year. All the deductions brought the average earnings of the stocking-weaver to four and sixpence per week. I found this to be a truth confirmed on every hand.

And when he was "in work", the man was evermore experiencing some new attempt at grinding him down to a lower sum per dozen for the weaving, or at "docking" him so much per dozen for alleged faults in his work; while sometimes—and even for several weeks together—he experienced the most grievous wrong of all. The "master" not being able to obtain full employment for all the frames he rented of the manufacturer, but perhaps only half employ for them—distributed, or "spread" the work over all the frames . . . But the foul grievance was this: each man had to pay a whole week's frame rent, although he had only half a week's work! Thus while the poor miserable weaver knew that his half-week's work, after all the deductions, would produce him such a mere pittance that he could only secure a scant share of the meanest food, he remembered that the owner of the frame had the full rent per week, and the middleman or "master" had also his weekly pickings secured to him.

from *Life*, 1872, by Thomas Cooper

Carding, drawing and roving cotton, 1835

Factories

. . . there are some branches of factory-work which have an especially injurious effect. In many rooms of the cotton and flax-spinning mills, the air is filled with fibrous dust, which produces chest affections, especially among workers in the carding and combing-rooms. Some constitutions can bear it, some cannot; but the operative has no choice. He must take the room in which he finds work, whether his chest is sound or not. The most common effects of this breathing of dust are blood-spitting, hard, noisy breathing, pains in the chest, coughs, sleeplessness—in short, all the symptoms of asthma ending in the worst cases in consumption. Especially unwholesome is the wet spinning of linen-yarn which is carried on by young girls and boys. The water spirts over them from the spindle, so that the front of their clothing is constantly wet through to the skin; and there is always water standing on the floor. This is the case to a less degree in the doubling-rooms of the cotton mills, and the result is a constant succession of colds and affections of the chest. A hoarse, rough voice is common to all operatives, but especially to wet spinners and doublers. Stuart, Mackintosh, and Sir D. Barry express themselves in the most vigorous terms as to the unwholesomeness of this work, and the small consideration shown by most of the manufacturers for the health of the girls who do it. Another effect of flax-spinning is a peculiar deformity of the shoulder, especially a projection of the right shoulder-blade, consequent upon the nature of the work. This sort of spinning and the throstle-spinning of cotton frequently produce diseases of the knee-pan, which is used to check the spindle during the joining of broken threads. The frequent stooping and the bending to the low machines common to both these branches of work have, in general, a stunting effect upon the growth of the operative. In the throstle-room of the cotton mill at Manchester, in which I was employed, I do not remember to have seen one single tall, well-built girl; they were all short, dumpy, and badly-formed, decidedly ugly in the whole development of the figure. But apart from all these diseases and malformations, the limbs of the operatives suffer in still another way. The work between the machinery gives rise to multitudes of accidents of more or less serious nature, which have for the operative the secondary effect of unfitting him for his work more or less completely. The most common accident is the squeezing off of a single joint of a finger, somewhat less common the loss of the whole finger, half or a whole hand, an arm, etc., in the machinery. Lockjaw very often follows, even upon the lesser among these injuries, and brings death with it. Besides the deformed persons, a great number of maimed ones may be seen going about in Manchester; this one has lost an arm or a part of one, that one a foot, this third half a leg; it is like living in the midst of an army just returned from a campaign. But the most dangerous portion of the machinery is the strapping which conveys motive power from the shaft to the separate machines, especially if it contains buckles, which, however, are rarely used now. Whoever is seized by the strap is carried up with lightning speed, thrown against the ceiling above and floor below with such force that there is rarely a whole bone left in the body, and death follows instantly. Between June 12th and August 3rd,

1843, the *Manchester Guardian* reported the following serious accidents (the trifling ones it does not notice): June 12th, a boy died in Manchester of lockjaw, caused by his hand being crushed between wheels. June 16th, a youth in Saddleworth seized by a wheel and carried away with it; died, utterly mangled. June 29th, a young man at Green Acres Moor, near Manchester, at work in a machine shop, fell under the grindstone, which broke two of his ribs and lacerated him terribly. July 24th, a girl in Oldham died, carried around fifty times by a strap; no bone unbroken. July 27th, a girl in Manchester seized by the blower (the first machine that receives the raw cotton), and died of injuries received. August 3rd, a bobbins turner died in Dukenfield, caught in a strap, every rib broken. In the year 1843, the Manchester Infirmary treated 962 cases of wounds and mutilations caused by machinery, while the number of all other accidents within the district of the hospital was 2,426, so that for five accidents from all other causes, two were caused by machinery. The accidents which happened in Salford are not included here, nor those treated by surgeons in private practice. In such cases, whether or not the accident unfits the victim for further work, the employer, at best, pays the doctor, or, in very exceptional cases, he may pay wages during treatment; what becomes of the operative afterwards, in case he cannot work, is no concern of the employer.

from *Conditions of the Working Classes in England*, 1844,
by Friedrich Engels

A collier and John Blenkinsop's locomotive of 1812

A Scottish Miner's Report

LORD ELCHO: What year was it in which you entered the mines?

ALEXANDER MACDONALD: About the year 1835 I think; I could not
fix the year. When I entered the mines at eight years of age or so,
at that time workings were not so large for we had not sunk in
Scotland to the thicker seams which are now being worked.

ELCHO: What mine did you enter?

MACDONALD: A mine called the Dyke Head Ironstone Mine.

ELCHO: Not a coal mine?

MACDONALD: Not a coal mine at first.

ELCHO: Where is that mine?

MACDONALD: In Lanarkshire.

ELCHO: Does that mine still exist?

MACDONALD: It does not exist now, it has long since been closed.
The condition of the miner's boy then was to be raised about
1 o'clock or 2 o'clock in the morning if the distance was very far
to travel, and I at that time had to travel a considerable distance,

68

more than three miles; I was raised at that time at 2 o'clock, and never later than 3 o'clock.

ELCHO: Do you mean that someone went round the place to call the boys?

MACDONALD: No. The men lived more then in their own cottages in that part of the country. We got up in the morning, I being called by my father at 1, or very often at 2 o'clock. We remained then in the mine until 5 and 6 at night. It was an ironstone mine, very low, working about 18 inches, and in some instances not quite so high.

ELCHO: That is, you remained 16 or 17 hours in the pit?

MACDONALD: Yes, as a rule.

ELCHO: Was the work constant for a boy of that age for that time?

MACDONALD: The work was perfectly constant.

ELCHO: No break?

MACDONALD: No break. Then I removed to coal mines after that. There we had low seams also, very low seams. There we had no rails to draw upon, that is, tramways laid like rails now for our tubs, or corves, or whirlies as we call them, to run upon. We had leather belts for our shoulders. One was before and another behind, and the wheels were cutting the pavements or floor (we called it pavement) and we had to keep dragging the coal with these ropes over our shoulders, and sometimes round the middle with a chain between our legs. Then there was always another behind pushing with his head.

ELCHO: That work was done with children?

MACDONALD: That work was done by boys, such as I was, from 10 or 11 down to eight, and I have known them as low as seven years old. In the mines at that time the state of ventilation was frightful.

MR MATHEWS: Are you now speaking of ironstone mines or coal mines?

MACDONALD: Of coal and ironstone mines together. The gases pervading the mines in Scotland at that time were, for the most part, carbonic acid gas, not carburetted hydrogen; and I remember well often having three or four lamps put together for the purpose of keeping so much light as to enable us to see by. A very great deal of our drawing, as we call it, was performed in the dark in consequence of the want of ventilation in the mines.

ELCHO: Did that want of ventilation at that time lead to frequent accidents?

MACDONALD: It did not lead to frequent accidents; but it led to premature death.

ELCHO: Not to explosion?

MACDONALD: No; carbonic acid gas in no case leads to explosion. There was no explosive gas in those mines I was in, or scarcely any. I may state incidentally here that in the first ironstone mine I was in there were some 20 or more boys besides myself, and I am not aware at this moment that there is one alive excepting myself.

Evidence given by Alexander MacDonald, 28th April, 1868, to *The Royal Commission on Trades Unions*

A Chartist Hymn

God of the Poor! shall labour eat?
Or drones alone find labour sweet?
Lo, they who call the earth their own,
Take all we have,—and give a stone!

Yet bring not thou on them the doom
That scourged the proud of wretched Rome,
Who stole, for few, the lands of all,
To make all life a funeral.

Lord! not for vengeance rave the wrong'd,
The hopes deferred, the woes prolonged;
Our cause is just, our Judge divine;
But judgement, God of all, is thine!

from *Corn Law Rhymes*, c. 1830, by Ebenezer Elliot

The Cropper Lads

Come crop-per lads of high re-nown, Who love to drink good ale that's brown, And strike each haugh-ty ty - rant down, With hatchet, pike and gun.

CHORUS

O, the crop-per lads for me, The gal - lant lads for me, Who with lus - ty stroke, the shear frames broke, The crop-per lads for me!

What though the specials still advance,
And soldiers nightly round us prance;
The cropper lads still lead the dance,
With hatchet, pike, and gun.

And night by night when all is still
And the moon is hid behind the hill,
We forward march to do our will
With hatchet, pike, and gun!

Great Enoch* still shall lead the van.
Stop him who dare! Stop him who can!
Press forward every gallant man,
With hatchet, pike, and gun!

a Luddite song from the early years
of the nineteenth century

* a large hammer produced by the firm of Enoch & James Taylor.

71

DEATH or LIBERTY! or Britannia & the Virtues of the Constitution in danger of Violation from the ge Tidskut Libertine, Radical Reform

"Death or Liberty!" by George Cruikshank

Resolutions of the London Corresponding Society
(*adopted at "The Bell", Exeter Street, Strand, 2nd April, 1792*)

Man as an individual is entitled to liberty, it is his Birth-right.

As a member of society the preservation of that liberty becomes his indispensable duty.

When he associated he gave up certain rights, in order to secure the possession of the remainder;

But, he voluntarily yielded up only as much as was necessary for the common good:

He still preserved a right of sharing the government of his country;—without it no man can, with truth, call himself *free*.

Fraud or force, sanctioned by custom, with-holds the right from (by far) the greater number of the inhabitants of this country.

The few with whom the right of election and representation remains abuse it, and the strong temptations held out to electors, sufficiently prove that the representatives of this country seldom procure a seat in parliament from the unbought suffrages of a free People.

The nation, at length, perceives it, and testifies an ardent desire of remedying the evil.

The only difficulty then, at present, is, the ascertaining the true method of proceeding.

To this end, different, and numerous Societies have been formed in different parts of the nation.

Several likewise have arisen in the Metropolis, and among them (though as yet in its infant state), the Corresponding Society, with modesty intrudes itself and opinions, on the attention of the public in the following resolutions:

Resolved,—That every individual has a right to share in the government of that society of which he is a member—unless incapacitated.

Resolved,—That nothing but non-age, privation of reason, or an offence against the general rules of society can incapacitate him.

Resolved,—That it is no less the *right* than the *duty* of every Citizen, to keep a watchful eye on the government of his country; that the laws, by being multiplied, do not degenerate into *oppression*, and that those who are entrusted with the government, do not substitute private interest for public advantage.

Resolved,—That the people of Great Britain are not effectually represented in Parliament.

Resolved,—That in consequence of a partial, unequal, and therefore inadequate representation, together with the corrupt method in which representatives are elected; oppressive taxes, unjust laws, restrictions of liberty, and wasting the public money have ensued.

Resolved,—That the only remedy for those evils is a fair, equal and impartial representation of the People in Parliament.

Resolved,—That a fair, equal, and impartial representation of the People in Parliament can never take place until all partial privileges are abolished.

Resolved,—That this Society do express their *abhorrence* of tumults and violence, and that, as they aim at reform, not anarchy, but reason, firmness, and unanimity, are the only arms they themselves will employ, or persuade their Citizens to exert against the Abuse of Power.

Ordered,—That the Secretary of this Society do transmit a copy of the above to the Societies.

from *Minute Book of the London Corresponding Society*, 2nd April, 1792

A Speech from the Throne, To the Senate of Lunataria In the Moon

My L-rds and G-tl-n,
    I grieve to say,
    That poor old Dad,
    Is just as—bad,
As when I met you here
    the other day.

'Tis pity that these cursed State Affairs
Should take you from your pheasants and your hares
        Just now:
        But lo!
CONSPIRACY and TREASON are abroad!
Those imps of darkness, gender'd in the wombs
Of spinning-jennies, winding-wheels, and looms,
        In Lunashire—
        Oh, Lord!
My L-rds and G-tl-n, we've much to fear!

Reform, Reform, the swinish rabble cry—
Meaning, of course, rebellion, blood and riot—
Audacious rascals! you, my Lords, and I,
Know 'tis their duty to be starved in quiet:
But they have grumbling habits, incompatible
With the repose of *our* august community—
They see that good things are with *us* come-at-ible,
And therefore slyly watch their opportunity
        To get a share;

Yes, they declare
That we are not God's favorites alone—
That *they* have rights to food, and clothes, and air,
As well as you, the Brilliants of a throne!
Oh! indications foul of revolution—
The villains would destroy the Constitution!

from *The Man in the Moon*, 1820, by William Hone

Peterloo

A little before noon on the 16th August, the first body of reformers began to arrive on the scene of action, which was a piece of ground called St Petersfield, adjoining a church of that name in the town of Manchester. These persons bore two banners, surmounted with caps of liberty, and bearing the inscriptions—"No Corn Laws", "Annual Parliaments", "Universal Suffrage", "Vote by Ballot". Some of these flags after being paraded round the field, were planted in the cart on which the speakers stood, but others remained in different parts of the crowd. Numerous large bodies of reformers continued to arrive from the towns in the neighbourhood of Manchester till about one o'clock, all preceded by flags, and many of them in marching order, five deep. Two clubs of female reformers advanced, one of them numbering more than 150 members, and bearing a silk banner. One body of reformers timed their steps to the sound of a bugle, with much of a disciplined air. . . . A band of special constables assumed a position on the field without resistance. The congregated multitude now amounted to a number roundly computed at 80,000, and the arrival of the hero of the day was impatiently expected. At length Mr. Hunt made his appearance, and after a rapturous greeting was invited to preside; he signified his assent and mounting a scaffolding, began to harangue his admirers. He had not proceeded far, when the appearance of the yeomenry cavalry advancing toward the area in a brisk trot, excited a panic in the outskirts of the meeting. . . . The cavalry dashed into the crowd, making for the cart on which the speakers were placed. The multitude offered no resistance. The commanding officer then approaching Mr. Hunt, and brandishing his sword, told him he was his prisoner. Mr. Hunt, after enjoining the people to tranquillity, said that he would readily surrender to any civil officer on showing his warrant, and Mr. Nadin, the principal police officer, received him in charge. . . . A cry now rose among the military of, "Have at their flags," and they dashed down not only those in the cart but the others dispersed in the field; cutting to right and to left to get at them. The people began running in all directions; and from this moment the yeomenry lost all control of temper: numbers were trampled under the feet of men and horses; many, both men and women were cut down by sabres, several, and a peace officer and a female, slain on the spot. The whole number of persons injured amounted to between three and four hundred. The populace threw a few stones and brickbats in their retreat; but in less than ten minutes the ground was entirely cleared of its former occupants. Mr. Hunt was led to prison not without incurring considerable danger, and some injury on his way from the swords of the yeomenry and the bludgeons of peace officers; the broken staves of two of his banners were carried in mock procession before him. The magistrates directed him to be locked up in a solitary cell, and the other prisoners were confined with the same precaution.

from *Annual Register*, 1819

A Letter on behalf of the Prince Regent Concerning Peterloo

My lord,

Having laid before the Prince Regent the accounts transmitted to me from Manchester of the proceedings at that place on Monday last, I have been commanded by his royal highness to request that your lordship will express to the magistrates of the county palatine of Lancaster, who attended on that day, the great satisfaction derived by his royal highness from their prompt, decisive and efficient measures for the preservation of the public tranquillity; and likewise that your lordship will communicate to major Trafford his royal highness's high approbation of the support and assistance to the civil power afforded on that occasion by himself and the officers, non-commissioned officers and privates, serving under his command.

I have the honour, etc.—
Sidmouth

To the Earl of Derby, etc.

from *Annual Register*, 1819

The Trial after Peterloo

The deposition of Matthew Cowper, was then read at the table. He stated the nature of the meeting; gave a history of the proceedings; and produced his notes of the commencement of a speech purporting to have been delivered by Mr Hunt at the meeting. Witness also deposed that he attended on the field at twelve at noon; that by that time half of the assemblage had collected; that most of the persons who composed it, carried large sticks, more like flails than walking sticks; that they advanced in military array, with flags and music; that one of the flags had upon it "No Corn Laws", and, on the other side a bloody dagger. The flags were in all sixteen, and there were five caps of liberty.

Witness examined by Mr Hunt.—Where do you reside, sir?

Witness.—In Manchester.

Mr Hunt.—Would you favour me with your particular address?

The bench, through its chairman again interfered, and would not allow the witness to answer the question. It was sufficient for the witness to declare he lived in Manchester.

Mr Hunt.—I demand as an act of justice, to know the residence of this man. It will be observed that he is a very material witness, and that his evidence may deeply affect us all. I am entitled to know where to find him, that if, after the trial in question, it shall be found there was no ground for this charge, I may have my remedy against him by a prosecution for perjury, or some other redress. I demand, therefore, as a right, to know his residence. (Mr

77

Hunt uttered this with considerable violence of voice and gesture.)

The magistrates consulted a minute, and then through their chairman, decided against complying with the demand. The chairman said there was no occasion for Mr Hunt to use intimidating language: it was not necessary to reiterate the word 'demand', to obtain that justice to which every British subject was entitled, and which might be obtained by a simple request. He further stated that he did not think it was treating the court with sufficient respect, to talk of demanding, as there was no disposition to refuse what was right, and no chance of obtaining what was wrong, by the use of strong terms.—The request of the prisoner would go as far as his demand. The court had considered the nature of the question put to the witness, and did not think it necessary that he should give his particular address: the description that he lived in Manchester and was an accountant, was quite sufficient.

Mr Hunt begged leave to reply to the observations of the chairman.

Chairman.—The court will not be replied to.

Mr Hunt.—I was merely about to state, that I had no intention of offering any insult to the court.

Chairman.—The court takes it for granted that you did not, and requires not any apology.

Mr Hunt.—I offered no insult to the court: when the witness refused to answer the question, I appealed to the court, and requested that he might be ordered to answer. I put this question in the shape of a demand, because I will not accept of anything as a favour. Addressing himself to the witness.—Now, of what profession are you?

Witness.—I am called an accountant.

Mr Hunt.—Is that your only occupation?

Chairman.—Don't answer that question.

Mr Hunt.—Were you a special constable, on Monday, the 16th, at the meeting?

Chairman.—Don't answer that question.

Mr Hunt, with great vehemence and apparent surprise.—Not answer that question? Have you any other employment than that of an accountant? Are you not sometimes employed as a short hand writer?

Witness.—I sometimes take reports of speeches.

78

Mr Hunt.—For the public newspapers, or for your own private amusement?

Chairman.—Don't answer that question.

Mr Hunt.—Then you say that you took my speech on the day of the meeting: did you take it in short hand, or otherwise?

Witness.—I took extracts from it on the ground and afterwards wrote it out at length. I only took the leading words. I do not mean to swear to all the words.

Mr Hunt.—Are you sure you did not misplace the words, putting some which you had in one sentence, into another?

Witness replied in the negative.

Mr Hunt.—How did you make out the remainder of the sentence from those extracts and leading words of yours?

I filled it up from memory.

When did you write out this speech from memory?

In the evening.

At what time was it delivered?

About one o'clock.

At what hour then, did you reduce your short notes into long sentences?

About five o'clock at night.

Be so good as to state how you were employed in the interval?

The chairman would not allow the witness to answer the question.

Mr Hunt remarked with considerable asperity on this interference, saying, it was important that an answer should be obtained. The witness stated that a very considerable interval had intervened between the delivery of the speech, and the preparation of his version of it; and that in the meantime he had entrusted a considerable part of it to his memory. The retentiveness of his memory would, of course, be affected by the importance of the other events in which he had been engaged, and therefore it was but just that he should state how he had been employed.

The court over-ruled this demand.

Mr Hunt to witness.—You state that you saw certain flags and colours, and that there was one of them with a bloody dagger; now what was there besides the bloody dagger?

The witness said he observed nothing else.

Mr Hunt.—Did you not observe a figure of justice, with the

scales in one hand, and a dagger, which you call a bloody dagger, in the other?

Witness replied in the negative.

Mr Hunt.—Will you swear there was nothing else.

Witness said he could not swear there was nothing else.

Mr Hunt.—You said you saw military array; what do you mean by military array?

Witness.—I mean people marching in regular order, as regiments march.

Have you no benefit societies in Manchester? Have you not orange clubs?

The court interfered, and said these questions were quite irrelevant. Mr Hunt contended that they were quite to his purpose, for when the witness spoke of regular order being miltary array, it was proper to call to his mind instances in which the former might occur without the latter. Then addressing himself to the witness, he asked,

Did you ever see benefit clubs marching with music and banners?

The witness said he had.

Have you not seen them marching in regular order?

The court interfered, and declared the question irrelevant. The chairman said that in interrupting the prisoner in these various questions, he and the other gentlemen acted on their best discretion.

Mr Hunt to the witness.—You said that the sticks you saw in the hands of the persons who came to the meeting were more like threshing flails than walking sticks; pray what do you mean by a flail? and what is the difference between it and a walking stick?

The chairman prevented the witness from answering the question.

Mr Hunt.—I was anxious to obtain an answer, because had I been allowed to go on, I should have drawn from the witness that there was nothing more common to the country people, than to use their old flails for walking sticks.—Addressing the witness.—Pray how were these sticks held?

They were shouldered like muskets.

Many other questions were put by Mr Hunt to this witness, but nothing very important was elicited.

from *Passages in the Life of a Radical*, 1839, by Samuel Bamford

"A Free Born Englishman!" by George Cruikshank

The Need for Parliamentary Reform

A stranger, who was told that this country is unparalleled in wealth and industry, and more civilized, and more enlightened than any country before it; that it is a country that prides itself on its freedom and that once in every seven years it elects representatives from its population, to act as the guardians and preservers of that freedom,— would be anxious and curious to see how that that representation is formed, and how the people chose those representatives, to whose faith and guardianship they entrust their free and liberal institutions. Such a person would be very much astonished if he were taken to a ruined mound, and told that that mound sent two representatives to Parliament—if he were taken to a park, where no houses were to be seen, and told that that park sent two representatives to Parliament; but if he were told all this, and were astonished at hearing it, he would be still more astonished if he were to see large and opulant towns full of enterprise and industry, . . . and were then told that these towns sent no representatives to Parliament.

Such a person would be still more astonished, if he were taken to Liverpool, where there is a large constituency, and told, here you will have a fine specimen of a popular election.

He would see bribery employed to the greatest extent, and in the most unblushing manner; he would see every voter receiving a number of guineas in a box, as the price of his corruption; and after such a spectacle, he would no doubt be much astonished that a nation whose representatives are thus chosen, could perform the functions of legislation at all, or enjoy respect in any degree. I say, then, that if the question before the House is a question of reason, the present state of representation is against reason.

The confidence of the country in the construction and constitution of the House of Commons is gone. . . . If, therefore, the question is one of right, right is in favour of Reform; if it be a question of reason, reason is in favour of Reform; if it be a question of policy and expediency, policy and expediency are in favour of Reform.

speech by Lord John Russell
on introduction of the First Reform Bill, 1st March, 1831

ERAL
.delaide-

1.

ic

s become
e for the
hich are

ily after
himself
Deferred,

e Policy
portional
either by
: Premi-

itable to
ly.
berland-

l Officer,
to Two
Y in at-
may be

AVEL-
fe Assur-
ed Tra-

CORONATION OF HER MAJESTY QUEEN VICTORIA THIS DAY.

This being the day appointed for the coronation of her Most Gracious Majesty Queen VICTORIA, long before dawn— the early dawn of a summer's day—the metropolis, it might literally be said, was in motion. Never within memory was London so full of strangers of illustrious birth, rank, title, and affluence as at the present moment, and all of our own nobility, and nearly the whole gentry of the United Kingdom, are also in town.

The whole line along which the procession passed was early crowded with multitudes of people of all classes and every age. The line of houses on both sides was fitted-up, with hardly an exception, with balconies and other suitable stations for seeing the procession go by.

STATE OF THE METROPOLIS THIS MORNING

For the last two or three days the numbers of persons that have been arriving by the coaches from all parts of the United Kingdom have given the streets of London an unusually full and animated appearance. but the most singular feature perhaps which presented itself to the eye of the observer among the moving mass, was the healthful ruddy cheeks visible in almost every direction, and which plainly told that the owners of " that same" were not residents of the great metropolis. This was equally manifest. too, from the wandering eye which devoured with so much avidity all that came within the scope of its vision, and the joyous anticipation of a great sight and a great treat which was expressed in every countenance. Although this has been more or less manifest for some days past, it was not until yesterday that the numbers of our visitors in London became so overwhelming as to render the streets altogether impassable. at least at the business-like pace which marks the gait of all true Londoners with the exception of a few west end idlers and fashionable strollers. From noon until late last night all the principal thoroughfares were crowded, while the streets forming the line of procession were literally blocked up.

from *The Globe*, 28th June, 1838

"The Penny Wedding" by David Wilkie

Robert Owen and New Lanark

He materially shortened the hours of labour from what they once had been. For the health and recreation of both old and young, he ordered walks to be cut at much personal expense, through the roads and fields surrounding that happy village. He entirely freed the people there, from all burden in paying the doctor's fees; he gratuitously gave to about five hundred children a useful and genteel education; he even at one time clothed the whole of these children in a beautiful dress of tartan cloth, fashioned in its make after the form of the Roman toga. To have seen these children at that time, so well attired and so happy, would have forced his bitterest enemies to have laid aside their enemity, and to have confessed he was a good man.

And permit me here just to say a little respecting the real blessings and advantages that belong to that school. The building itself is a stately edifice; if I mistake not, it is 100 feet long by 50 feet broad, and I believe cost about £6,000. There are in it five principal rooms; two of these are employed as apartments for reading and writing, two of them as dancing rooms, and one as an infant school. In the south flat is a large apartment fitted up with elegant and usefully-constructed bathing machines, for the purpose of promoting the health and cleanliness of the children. . . . There is dancing, drawing, vocal and instrumental music, with knitting and sewing for the girls, also taught; and I may mention that while I was employed in that institution, the teachers were, as I have said before, almost all members of the Church of Scotland, which shews to the world more than anything else, one would think, that Mr. Owen was far from attempting to palm upon the youth of that neighbourhood his peculiar dogmas [Owen was an atheist].

from *R. Owen at New Lanark by One formerly a Teacher at New Lanark*, 1839

Postscript

And Did Those Feet in Ancient Time

And did those feet in ancient time
Walk upon England's mountains green?
And was the holy Lamb of God
On England's pleasant pastures seen?

And did the Countenance Divine
Shine forth upon our clouded hills?
And was Jerusalem builded here
Among these dark Satanic mills?

Bring me my bow of burning gold!
Bring me my arrows of desire!
Bring me my spear! O clouds unfold!
Bring me my chariot of fire!

I will not cease from mental fight,
Nor shall my sword sleep in my hand
Till we have built Jerusalem
In England's green and pleasant land.

from preface to *Milton*, 1804, by William Blake

Further Source Material

Literature

SAMUEL BAMFORD   *Passages in the Life of a Radical*   MacGibbon & Kee
WILLIAM BRANCH-JOHNSON   *The Carrington Diary, 1797–1810*
                      C. Johnson
ASA BRIGGS   *The Age of Improvement*   Longman
SIR ARTHUR BRYANT   *The Age of Elegance*   Collins
JOHN CLIVE   *Scotch Reviewers: The "Edinburgh Review", 1802–15*   Faber
WILLIAM COBBETT   *The Autobiography of William Cobbett: The Progress
              of a Plough-boy to a Seat in Parliament*   Faber
              Rural Rides   Penguin
THOMAS CREEVEY   *The Creevey Papers* (ed. by John Gore)   Batsford
LLOYD EVANS and PHILIP PLEDGER   *Contemporary Sources and Opinions
                      in Modern British History* (in 2
                      vols)   Warne
RONALD FLETCHER   *The Parkers at Saltram, 1769–89: Everyday Life in
              an Eighteenth-Century House*   B.B.C.
JONATHAN GOODMAN (ed.)   *Bloody Versicles: The Rhymes of Crime*
               David & Charles
HELEN GRAHAM   *Parties and Pleasures: The Diaries of Helen Graham,
            1823–1826* (ed. by James Irvine)   Paterson
CHARLES CAVENDISH FULKE GREVILLE   *The Greville Memoirs* (ed. by
                             Roger Fulford)   Batsford
GEOFFREY GRIGSON (ed.)   *Unrespectable Verse*   Allen Lane
IAN GRIMBLE   *Regency People*   B.B.C.
ROGER W. HART   *English Life in the Eighteenth Century*   Wayland
           English Life in the Nineteenth Century   Wayland
CHRISTOPHER HARVIE, GRAHAM MARTIN   *Industrialisation and Culture,*
and AARON SCHARF (eds)   *1830–1914*   Macmillan for
               the Open University
ERIC HOBSBAWM and GEORGE RUDÉ   *Captain Swing*   Laurence and
               Wishart (*also* Penguin)
FRANK EDWARD HUGGETT   *What They've Said About Nineteenth-Century
              Statesmen: A Selection of Source Material*
              O.U.P.
              *What They've Said About Nineteenth-Century
              Reformers: A Selection of Source Material*
              O.U.P.
FRANCIS D. KLINGENDER   *Art and the Industrial Revolution*   Evelyn,
              Adams & MacKay (*also* Paladin)

JAMES LAVER *The Age of Optimism: Manners and Morals, 1848–1914*
  Weidenfeld & Nicolson
MARGOT LISTER *Costumes of Everyday Life: An Illustrated History of
  Working Clothes from 900 to 1910* Barrie & Jenkins
WILLIAM LOVETT *Life and Struggles* MacGibbon & Kee
STELLA MARGETSON *Leisure and Pleasure in the Nineteenth Century*
  Cassell
JOYCE MARLOW *The Peterloo Massacre* Rapp & Whiting (*also* Panther)
FRANCIS PLACE *The Autobiography of Francis Place* Cambridge U.P.
DONALD READ *The Peterloo Massacre and its Background* Manchester
  U.P.
EDGELL RICKWORD (ed.) *Radical Squibs and Loyal Ripostes: Satirical
  Pamphlets of the Regency Period, 1819–1821*
  Adams and Dart
EDWARD PALMER THOMPSON *The Making of the English Working Class*
  Penguin
JOHN WARDROPER *Kings, Lords and Wicked Libellers: Satire and Protest,
  1760–1837* J. Murray
ELLIS WATERHOUSE *Painting in Britain, 1530 to 1790* Penguin
REGINALD JAMES WHITE *Life in Regency England* Batsford
T. HANBURY WHITE *The Age of Scandal* Penguin
MERRYN WILLIAMS (ed.) *Revolutions, 1775–1830* Penguin for the Open
  University
DOREEN YARWOOD *The English Home* Batsford

Museums of Special Interest

Ironbridge Gorge Museum
Coalbrookdale Museum and Furnace Site } Shropshire
Blist's Hill Open Air Museum
The Science Museum, London
Castle Museum, York
North of England Open Air Museum, Beamish, Co. Durham
Dorset County Museum, Dorchester
Royal Scottish Museum, Edinburgh
Gladstone Court, Biggar, Lanarkshire
Lewis Textile Museum, Blackburn, Lancashire
Sticklepath, near Okehampton, Devon